W9-BNN-549

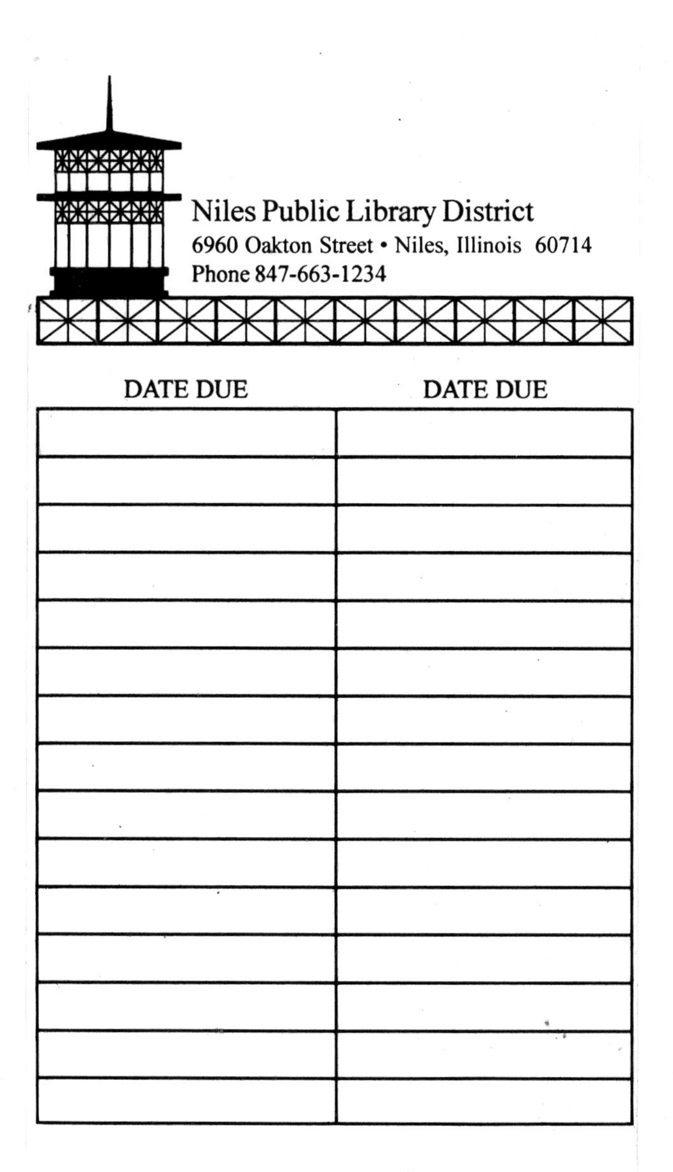
Niles Public Library District
6960 Oakton Street • Niles, Illinois 60714
Phone 847-663-1234
DATE DUE
DATE DUE

BLACK ✦ STARS

AFRICAN AMERICAN MUSICIANS

✦

ELEANORA E. TATE

JIM HASKINS, GENERAL EDITOR

John Wiley & Sons, Inc.
New York • Chichester • Weinheim • Brisbane • Singapore • Toronto

This book is printed on acid-free paper. ♾

Published by John Wiley & Sons, Inc.
Published simultaneously in Canada
Design and production by Navta Associates, Inc.

Library of Congress Cataloging-in-Publication Data

Tate, Eleanora E.
African American musicians / by Eleanora E. Tate ; Jim Haskins, general editor.
p. cm. — (Black stars series)
Includes bibliographical references and index.
Summary: Presents biographical profiles of African Americans, both legendary and less well-known, who have made significant contributions to music in the United States over the past 200 years.
ISBN 0-471-25356-1 (cloth : alk. paper)
1. Afro-American musicians—Biography—Juvenile literature. [1. Musicians. 2. Afro-Americans—Biography.] I. Haskins, James, 1941– II. Title. III. Black stars (New York, N.Y.)

ML3929 .T38 2000
780'.92'396073—dc21

99-051360

Printed in the United States of America
10 9 8 7 6 5 4 3 2 1

Contents

To Frances Hawthorne, who taught me how to write my first newspaper article at the *Iowa Bystander* newspaper in 1966; Joan Bunke, who faithfully supplied me with so many books on these legendary greats for so many years during and after my R&T days in the 1960s, 1970s, 1980s, and even in the 1990s; to Nick Baldwin, who generously gave me so many wonderful albums back in those R&T years; to the late James B. Morris Sr., my first boss at the *Iowa Bystander* in 1966, who believed that I could write; to my husband, Zack Hamlett III, who knows music much better than I ever will; to our daughter Gretchen, whom I will always dearly love with all my heart, despite my many motherly mistakes; and to James Haskins, who so kindly gave me this opportunity.

ACKNOWLEDGMENTS

I could not have written *African American Musicians* had I not had such excellent support from Carole Hall, editor in chief of the African American program at John Wiley, and her assistant, Carrette Perkins, who kept me going when I often feared that I was in way over my head.

In addition to my husband and best friend, Zack E. Hamlett III, and to so many sympathetic friends, including Beverly Fields Burnette, Darby West, Cheryl Mosley, and Emily and Winston Collymore, I am extremely grateful to the following people, libraries, museums, and their staffs who offered me tremendous research opportunities:

Mrs. Violet Bailey of Beaufort, N.C., for information on the Menhaden Chanteymen; Wanda Cox-Bailey, branch manager, and her staff at the Richard B. Harrison Library, Raleigh, N.C., and its sister branches in the Wake County (N.C.) Library system; the Kansas City (Mo.) Public Library; the Kansas City (Mo.) Jazz Museum; Dr. Pauletta Bracy and North Carolina Central University's Shepherd Library, Durham; Dr. Nancy Shawcros and the University of Pennsylvania special library for its Marian Anderson collection, Philadelphia; Onslow County (N.C.) library system; Morehead State University Library, Morehead, Minn.; Iowa City Music Library, Iowa City, Iowa; New Hanover County Library, Wilmington, N.C.; personal interviews with Ray Charles, Ron and Natalie Daise, Doug and Frankie Quimby; Sandy Myers; Dr. Nancy Tolson; Brenda McDonald, Director of Central Services, St. Louis (Mo.) Public Library; Leroy Henderson, Education Director, Chattanooga (Tenn.) African American Museum; Missouri Historical Society Research Library, St. Louis; authors and researchers Gary Giddins and Tom Morgan; Tanya Farrar, Annette Davis, and the Carteret Community College Library–Learning Resources Center, Morehead City, N.C.; Whiteville (N.C.) County

Library and the North Carolina Department of Cultural Resources, Division of Archives and History, Raleigh, for archival information on Millie-Christine McCoy; Michael Cogswell and George Arevalo, Queens College for the Louis Armstrong Museum; Thais St. Julien and the Maxwell Music Library, Tulane University, New Orleans; the Rock and Roll Hall of Fame and Museum, Cleveland, Ohio; the W. C. Handy Birthplace, Museum, and Library, Florence, Alabama; Dr. Harry Robinson and Daphne Stephenson of the Dallas African American Museum; and Lori Chambers, Editor, *Rutgers* magazine.

INTRODUCTION

✦

America's major musical gifts to the world were created in African American neighborhoods. These gifts include spirituals, gospels, ragtime, blues, jazz, rhythm and blues, rock and roll, even hip-hop. All found their beginnings in the homes and communities in the United States where the sons and daughters of Africa lived:

In Georgia's slave quarters. In Tennessee's sharecropper shanties. On Harlem's 125th Street, and in New Orleans's Storyville red-light district. On Kansas City's Eighteenth and Vine and Memphis's Beale Street. In Alabama's cotton and tobacco fields, the Mississippi Delta, and Florida and Texas juke joints. In New York brownstones, Philadelphia and Harlem churches, and Baltimore row houses. On St. Louis Mississippi River levees, in Chicago's South Side public housing projects, and in proper middle-class parlors east, west, north, and south. Wonderful music emerged from the artists living in or escaping from these environments. Wherever black musicians went, their music retained their unique flavorings of home, love, God, and hope and carried their messages to the world. Their musical expressions give us a unique perspective on American history from its beginnings to the present day.

African American music began with African people's unconquerable spirit and will to survive in a new land despite enslavement. Slave traders who ripped the sons and daughters of Africa from their beds and villages also separated them from most of their physical belongings. Most had to leave without even a comb. But the African's drum was allowed to come: the slave traders thought music and dancing would keep their stolen cargo happy and docile. When they discovered that the drum was the major means of communication among the Africans, whose many languages kept them apart, the drum, too, was banned.

But even without a physical drum, these heroic peoples kept the memories of their families and their music with them. Their bodies and their voices became their musical instruments until they could build their own again. They also found spiritual sustenance in memories of their traditional gods, and in the promise of freedom through the god they were taught to worship in America.

Strengthened spiritually and mentally by their memories and new beliefs, they were able to endure and survive their troubles by praising their god through song, with rhythm supplied by clapping their hands and moving their feet. Those songs became "plantation songs," "slave songs," "jubilee songs," work songs, and spirituals, created by many unknown individuals inspired by God and biblical stories.

Slaveholders who allowed their slaves to worship as Christians tried to control how they did it. But determined to sing and "hold praise in their own way,"[1] slaves would "huddle behind soaking wet quilts and rags that had been hung to form a sort of tabernacle"[2] to muffle the sound. Other times, they would "take an iron pot or kettle, turn it upside down, place it in the middle of the cabin floor or at the door step, then prop it up slightly to hold the sound."[3]

The oldest African American music is the most enduring. It contains the most compelling messages for freedom. Spirituals such as "Go Down, Moses"; "Didn't My Lord Deliver Daniel?"; "Swing Low, Sweet Chariot"; "Steal Away"; and "This Little Light of Mine" were "seeking-emancipation songs" from slavery. African Americans developed this music during colonial times and during the Civil War years. But even after emancipation, they were not really free. So the spirituals remained as meaningful as they were beautiful. Black musicians like the Fisk Jubilee Singers and concert singers like Matilda Joyner (also known as Sissieretta Jones) made these songs popular with a wide audience outside the South following the Civil War.

Deep into the twentieth century, great black singers such as Roland Hayes, Paul Robeson, Marian Anderson, and Jessye Norman kept the old songs alive in concerts and churches. Some of the spirituals became the "freedom songs" of the civil rights movements of the 1950s and 1960s.

Along the way, African Americans invented new musical forms. When slave songs, spirituals, work songs, and chanties came together at the turn of century, the new sounds of gospel, ragtime, and blues were born. African Americans continued to improvise and create new ways of expressing themselves through their music, and in modern times have given us the unforgettable sounds of jazz, rock and roll, soul, and rap.

Throughout history, African American musicians contributed to many of the musical traditions of the world. Some of the earliest African American musicians performed European classical music. You will find African American musicians bringing their unique talents to classical music today as well as to Latin-flavored music and all types of American popular music.

African American Musicians is a collection of some of these surprising black stars in American history. It includes those whose drumbeats and voices first sounded on American soil centuries ago as well as those we see, hear, and admire today. Some are singers. Others play instruments, lead bands and orchestras, or write the music itself. May all of their bright lights shine forever.

Part One

✦

The Early Years

ELIZABETH TAYLOR GREENFIELD

(1809–1876)

Among the earliest African Americans to make a splash in American music was Elizabeth Taylor Greenfield. Despite the absence of a black role model in concert music, this dedicated black star became known around the world as an "African nightingale" for her remarkable singing voice.

Elizabeth Greenfield was born in Natchez, Mississippi, in 1809 to an enslaved couple named Taylor. Elizabeth's father was a native African. He and Elizabeth's mother lived on the homestead of Mrs. Holliday Greenfield, a wealthy woman from Philadelphia, Pennsylvania. Although Mrs. Greenfield was a Quaker, she owned slaves. When she decided to move back to Pennsylvania, she freed Elizabeth's parents and sent them to Liberia, but she kept baby Elizabeth. The child lived with Mrs. Greenfield for several years, then moved in with one of her own relatives, Mary Parker.

At a young age Elizabeth showed "a propensity for singing and probably did so at her local church."[1] By the time Elizabeth was in her late teens, she had a basic understanding of music and was

probably amazing her friends with her songs. In the meantime, Mrs. Greenfield had grown old. At Mrs. Greenfield's request, Elizabeth became her companion and live-in housekeeper, but she never stopped singing.

One of Mrs. Greenfield's neighbors, Miss Price, heard Elizabeth singing and was so impressed that she gave Elizabeth music lessons. Miss Price's interest in Elizabeth was valuable because it introduced Elizabeth to other whites who encouraged her with her music.

With Mrs. Greenfield's support, Elizabeth began singing at private parties in the Philadelphia area. Mrs. Greenfield died in the mid-1840s. Her will stated that $1,500 was to be set aside for the return of Elizabeth's mother from Liberia, and that $100 was to be given annually to Elizabeth throughout her lifetime. Mrs. Greenfield's relatives and attorneys, however, contested the will so vigorously that Elizabeth never received any money.

But the young songstress persevered. In 1849, Elizabeth received her first "break." A prominent Philadelphia musician and bandmaster hired her to sing in Baltimore. While in Baltimore, she also looked for jobs as a music teacher. When she heard that the "Swedish nightingale" Jenny Lind was scheduled to sing in Buffalo, New York, in 1851, Greenfield began saving her money to pay for her travel there. While on a boat en route to Buffalo, she met and sang for Buffalo resident Mrs. H. B. Potter, who invited her to sing for her friends at her Buffalo mansion.

A group of Buffalo residents sponsored Elizabeth in a series of concerts for the Buffalo Music Association. The first concert was held October 22, 1851. The concerts were so successful that Elizabeth was nicknamed the "Black Swan" after Jenny Lind. Greenfield went on to sing in nonslaveholding states and in Canada. She was a soprano whose range was over three and one-fourth octaves. She often amazed her audiences by singing the song "Old Folks at Home" first as a soprano, and then as a baritone.

- ✦ An **octave** is a whole series of eight notes.
- ✦ A **soprano** sings the highest notes.
- ✦ A **baritone** sings notes almost as low as a bass, who sings the lowest notes.

Despite her popularity, Greenfield suffered many instances of racism in the North. On March 31, 1853, for example, she was scheduled to sing at the Metropolitan Hall in New York before 4,000 people. No other black people were allowed. Someone threatened to "burn the house" if a "colored woman sang" there.[2] Police had to be brought in to protect the building. Greenfield sang, even though she was frightened. Mindful of the exclusion of her own people, she gave a follow-up concert to help the Home of Aged Colored Persons and the Colored Orphan Asylum.

That same year, she went to London, England, to sing, but had problems with the promoter over money. Author Harriet Beecher Stowe, who was in town at the same time to publicize her book *Uncle Tom's Cabin*, went to hear her sing. Stowe helped introduce Greenfield to the Duchess of Sutherland and to Sir George Smart, the Queen of England's musician. This led to more concerts, and Greenfield also received musical training from Sir George. On May 10, 1854, she gave a command performance at Buckingham Palace for England's Queen Victoria.

Queen Victoria said that Greenfield had "a most wonderful compass of voice, ranging over fully three octaves with fine, clear high notes. . . ."[3]

Upon Greenfield's return to the United States, she continued touring, sang again in Canada, and completed another tour of the northern United States in 1856. Between tours, she taught music to other rising stars in Philadelphia. She stopped touring when anti-black sentiment rose over the Dred Scott decision and the Civil War began. Her last extended tour was in 1863.

When Elizabeth Taylor Greenfield was not on the road, she was involved in social and religious activities in support of other African Americans, the homeless, the Freedman's Society, black churches, and orphans. She died in Philadelphia on March 31, 1876.

AN ENTERPRISING BLACK STAR

Elizabeth Taylor Greenfield not only organized a Black Swan Opera Troupe, but also wrote her autobiography, *The Black Swan at Home and Abroad,* or *A Biographical Sketch of Miss Elizabeth Taylor Greenfield, the American Vocalist.* It was privately printed in 1855.

EDMUND DEDE

(1827–1903)

Edmund Dede was born in New Orleans on November 20, 1827. His parents were free Creoles of color who had moved to New Orleans from the French West Indies around 1809. New Orleans, an aristocratic city since its earliest days, was an international seaport. Its population was primarily made up of French, English, Spanish, and Italian people, free black people, and enslaved Africans.

This variety of ethnic groups made for a rich mix. People of mixed heritage sometimes called themselves Creoles. Even among the Creoles, however, distinctions were made between white Creoles, Creoles of color, and light-skinned and dark-skinned Creoles. Some of the earliest composers of American music had this mixture of New Orleans roots.

Young Edmund, who was a dark-skinned Creole, first took music lessons from his father, a bandmaster for a local military group, and learned how to play the clarinet. He studied violin under Ludovico Gabici, a white teacher, and Christian Debergue, a free Creole of color. Charles Richard Lambert also instructed young Edmund. Lambert

was a New York–born free black musician, music teacher, and conductor of the New Orleans Free Creoles of Color Philharmonic Society.

From around 1848 to 1851, Edmund Dede lived in Mexico where he continued his musical education. Because of an illness, Dede returned to his hometown in 1851, where he created and probably published the piece "Mon Pauvre Coeur" (My Poor Heart), known to be the "oldest piece of sheet music by a New Orleans Creole of color."[1]

In 1857, with money saved from his job as a cigar-maker, Dede traveled to England and then to Paris, France, where he entered the Paris Conservatory for advanced musical study. From there, he worked as an orchestra conductor of the L'Alcazar in Bordeaux. Being in France was much like being back home for Dede because of New Orleans's French roots. Like many other free Louisiana Creoles of color who had moved to France, Dede also experienced less racial prejudice in France than he had in the United States. In 1864, he married a French woman named Sylvie Leflat.

Dede was a popular, prolific musician. While living in Bordeaux, for example, he wrote over 250 dances and songs, as well as numerous comic operas. He was also known for his ballet music, "Ables," "Les Faux Mandarins," and "La Sensitive." His overture "Le Palmier" was performed in New Orleans on August 22, 1865.

He returned to the United States in 1893 to visit relatives. The boat he was on wrecked in rough weather, and he lost his prized Cremona violin. He was rescued with the other passengers and taken to Galveston, Texas, where he was "acclaimed by the best musicians of that section, both white and black."[2] Dede traveled to several American cities, including Chicago, giving violin concerts, before returning to France in 1894. Edmund Dede died in 1903.

Part Two

✦

The Civil War Years and Reconstruction

THOMAS "BLIND TOM" GREENE

BETHUNE

(1849–1908)

Today, musicians with physical disabilities are acknowledged and respected. In past years, however, a talented musician with a disability was looked upon as an oddity. If the musician was also black and a slave, he or she was often exploited or, in extreme cases, treated cruelly. But the blind pianist and composer Thomas Greene Bethune rose above his limitations.

Bethune was known to millions of Americans and Europeans as "Blind Tom," the "human mockingbird." Tom had no formal schooling on the piano or in music. He would listen to the sounds in the countryside around him, memorize them, and play them back on the piano perfectly. Tom flabbergasted audiences with his talent for over thirty years.

Thomas was born sightless and into slavery to Charity Wiggins on May 25, 1849, on the Wiley Edward Jones plantation near Columbus, Georgia. Thomas, his mother, and his siblings were soon sold to a Columbus plantation owner named James N. Bethune.

BLIND TOMS
RAIN STORM

As a child, Thomas did not play much with other children. His playmate was the piano. When he was only four years old, he was discovered at the Bethune family piano, perfectly playing back songs he had heard. The technical term for this ability is "absolute pitch." Tom had a phenomenal musical memory. He would memorize and then re-create notes and songs of all the sounds he had heard from the trees, the wind, and the birds. Some said he could even reproduce the sound of thunder.

His talents shocked everyone, and James Bethune, being a capitalist, declared himself the manager of this "unusual" slave child. By age eight, young Tom was already performing at concerts that his master organized in the Columbus area. Bethune's wife was a music teacher, and she and her daughters would play piano selections by Bach, Beethoven, Chopin, Mendelssohn, and others for Thomas to play back. And he did, steadily increasing his repertoire.

In 1858, James Bethune hired Blind Tom out to a Georgia planter named Perry Oliver, who exhibited him as "the musical prodigy of the age: A Plantation Negro Boy." His first known New York concert was on January 15, 1861, just before the outbreak of the Civil War. Sadly, after the war began, Thomas was forced to give concerts for the same Confederate soldiers who were fighting to keep him and other African Americans enslaved.

✦ Your **repertoire** is the complete list of pieces you can perform.

✦ A **prodigy** is a young person who has extraordinary talents or abilities.

Blind Tom remained under Bethune's authority even after slavery and the war ended. Bethune had declared himself Tom's legal guardian and continued to collect whatever money the teenager earned.

Wherever Blind Tom played other musicians and nonbelievers in the audience would constantly test his competence. During his concerts, the audience would call out names of selections for him to play.

The Prodigy

Blind Tom Bethune knew how to play nearly 7,000 musical selections. He could play all types of music, from marches, dances, operas, and ballads to plantation songs. He even composed his own music, and published some under his name and others under the pseudonyms J. C. Beckel and François Sexalise. His best-known original piece was "Battle of Manassas," named after a Civil War battle.

Many came up on stage and played original work for him to repeat. Each time, Blind Tom would play back perfectly everything he had heard. "Once, while performing at the White House, he played correctly a twenty-page piece a short time after hearing it."[1]

Today, Thomas Bethune would be recognized as a master musician. But in a time when most whites believed African Americans to be inferior and less than human, his superior musical abilities made many consider him a freak. Some historians believed he suffered from a form of mental illness. What Thomas Bethune's feelings were about his life may never be known. He never reaped the financial rewards to which he was entitled, but he continued to perform for many years.

He gave concerts throughout America under the legal guardianship of James Bethune. After James Bethune died, his son, and then the son's widow continued to reap the financial rewards of Thomas's talents.

Blind Thomas Bethune died in poverty in 1908 in Hoboken, New Jersey. The Bethune family never freed their "human mockingbird." A marker placed where he was born near Columbus, Georgia, is on the list of state historic landmarks.

Millie-Christine McCoy

(1851–1912)

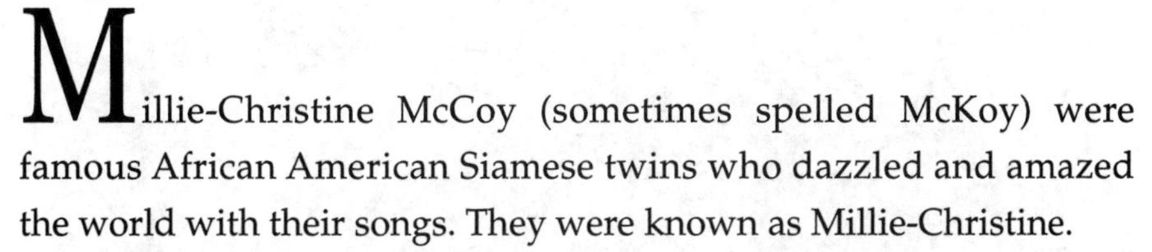

Millie-Christine McCoy (sometimes spelled McKoy) were famous African American Siamese twins who dazzled and amazed the world with their songs. They were known as Millie-Christine.

The twins were born as slaves on July 11, 1851, in the rural Welches Creek community near Whiteville, North Carolina. Their parents, Monemia and Jacob McCoy, were the slaves of plantation owner Jabez McCoy. McCoy sold the babies for $1,000 to John C. Purvis, who then sold them to J. P. Smith. Over the next several years, greedy white profiteers kidnapped them at least three times. At one time, the twins were stolen and were missing for three years before Smith finally found them in England. After a lengthy court trial that established Smith as their legal owner, the children were returned to him.

The little girls were subjected to numerous medical examinations. They were joined in the area of the hip and lower spine, but each child had the use of her own arms and legs. They possessed above-average intelligence, and played and acted like other children their age. In conversation, each preferred using "I" rather than "we" when

referring to themselves. Unlike Blind Tom Bethune, Millie-Christine enjoyed private tutors. They learned to dance and sing, and were well educated.

On posters and handbills, they were often billed as the "Carolina Nightingale" or the "United African Twins," with Christine singing soprano and Millie alto.[1] They sang with "rich, sweet voices" such popular songs of their time as "Old Black Joe," "The Whip-poor-will's Song," and "Listen to the Mocking Bird." Millie-Christine were fluent in seven languages and sang not only in English but in French as well.

By the end of the Civil War, Millie-Christine had gained their freedom but kept J. P. Smith as their manager. Circus showman P. T. Barnum was also one of their promoters. At the peak of their singing career, they performed before England's Prince of Wales and Queen Victoria, who was so impressed by their talents that she gave them matching diamond brooches. They sang before all the royal families of Europe, and visited forty-six American states, at one time earning more than $600 a week. When Millie-Christine were not traveling, they lived in a large house they had built on part of the old McCoy family homestead in Welches Creek, where they were born.

Described as charitable, religious, and gentle, Millie-Christine sang at fairs, in circuses, and at special activities until 1880, when they retired from full-time performing. They helped to establish an African American school in the Welches Creek community and gave generously to other North Carolina schools. Warm and friendly to everybody, the twins had special get-togethers with other African Americans on Sunday afternoons on their front porch.

In 1909, their beloved home burned to the ground. The twins lost nearly all of the large collection of memorabilia they had collected on their travels around the world, including the brooches given to them by Queen Victoria. They spent their remaining years in a nearby six-room cottage. On October 8, 1912, at age sixty-one, Millie died of tuberculosis. Christine died several hours later.

Millie-Christine had feared that after their death they would be dissected or placed on exhibit, so they requested that their bodies be cremated. Instead, they were buried in the family cemetery near their home. For nearly a year, guards remained near the cemetery to discourage grave robbers. Over the years, most people forgot about the famous twins.

In 1969, interest in Millie-Christine was renewed. With the assistance of the Columbus County Historical Society, the North Carolina State Department of Archives and History, and relatives, the twins' remains were moved during a ceremony to the Welches Creek Community Cemetery, three miles outside of Whiteville. Inscribed on their tombstone are the words "A soul with two thoughts. Two hearts that beat as one."[2]

A historical marker on North Carolina Highway 74–76 outside of Whiteville also honors the twins' achievements.

The Carolina Nightingale

When Millie-Christine received visitors on their front porch in North Carolina, they liked to recite a poem they had composed about their life. The final lines were

I'm happy quite, because content,
For some wise purpose I was sent;
My Maker knows what he has done,
Whether I'm created two or one.[3]

Part Three

✦

Into the New Century

SCOTT JOPLIN

(1868–1917)

At the turn of the century, a new musical style was born. It combined Mississippi River–town saloon tunes, European classical styles, the rhythm and swing of blackface minstrelsy, and African American work songs. Fast and hard-driving, it was called ragtime. The musician who popularized it was Scott Joplin.

Scott Joplin was born on November 24, 1868, near the Texas-Arkansas border. Some people say his birthplace is Texarkana, Texas. Others believe that he was born in Linden, Texas, then moved to Texarkana with his family when he was around seven years old. Scott was the son of freeborn Florence Givens Joplin, a laundress, and Giles (sometimes spelled Jiles) Joplin, a former slave. Scott was the second of six children.

The Joplin family was very musical. Scott's mother sang and played the guitar, and his father played the violin. They often performed at local weddings, parties, and funerals. Little Scott was attracted first to his mother's guitar, but then began teaching himself to play the piano. He also received free piano lessons from black music teachers

and from German-born Jacob Weiss, a local music teacher.[1] By the time Scott was eleven, he could improvise amazingly well and was often called a child prodigy.

✦ To **improvise** means to make something up on the spot.

Eager to make a living as a musician, young Joplin left home and began playing in honky-tonks, saloons, and taverns in the South, Southwest, and Midwest.

By 1897, he had moved to Sedalia, Missouri, where he learned music theory and harmony at the George S. Smith College for Negroes. He continued to write his own songs, and often played them on the piano at the two black social clubs in Sedalia, the Maple Leaf and the 400. A year later Joplin wrote "Maple Leaf Rag." In the fall of 1899, "Maple Leaf Rag" was published.

Joplin had once said that "Maple Leaf Rag" would one day make him the king of ragtime composers.[2] It did. The pianola, invented in 1900, was an early version of the player piano. The pianola dramatically increased the popularity of Joplin's music, especially his "Maple Leaf Rag." By 1909, the song had sold nearly 500,000 copies. Joplin earned one penny on every copy sold, a financial windfall for the times.

Known to be a quiet, modest, and very serious person, Joplin believed in the importance of education. He often tutored younger

Inventing a New Kind of Music

While working in a band at the Columbian Exposition during the 1893 Chicago world's fair, Scott met other musicians and was encouraged to write down his tunes. Unlike the white musicians, Scott and his new friends added lots of their own rhythms and beats to European songs and melodies. Soon, what had been called "raggin" became known as ragtime. And the beats were known as syncopation.

An early sheet-music cover for "Maple Leaf Rag," featuring a dedication to the Maple Leaf club that had inspired the ragtime song.

musicians and was active in local bands. In 1901, he and his wife Belle moved to St. Louis, where he wrote "The Entertainer" (1902) and other popular ragtime tunes. But Joplin had even bigger dreams.

Determined to prove, primarily to whites, that ragtime music was just as worthy of respect as was classical music, Joplin incorporated complex patterns and serious themes into his music. He wrote over sixty compositions, including two operas, a march, and a ragtime ballet titled *The Rag Time Dance.*

After his marriage to Belle ended, he married a young woman named Freddie Alexander and returned to Sedalia. Tragically, the new Mrs. Joplin became ill and died only three months after they were married.[3] Stunned, Joplin left Sedalia and returned to St. Louis. He traveled around for a short time, and finally moved to New York, where he married Lottie Stokes and continued to compose the music he loved.

He composed and financed his second opera, *Treemonisha*. The opera is about a girl named Treemonisha who wants to save her people. It takes place among black farmers in 1880s Arkansas, but with the same Texas setting where Joplin was born.[4] Because the opera was performed without the benefit of scenery, costumes, lighting, or an orchestra, it had a short life on the stage.

Depressed over the failure of *Treemonisha* to find a suitable audience, and disappointed in the waning interest in ragtime, Scott Joplin became ill. He died on April 1, 1917, in Manhattan State Hospital in New York City.

Joplin had always believed that one day his beloved ragtime would be respected, and he was right. Fifty-six years after his death, his song "The Entertainer" became a huge success. It was the theme song to the hit movie *The Sting*. And a prizewinning book and a play—both called *Ragtime*—would bring more fame and honor to his music in the 1980s and 1990s. The music lived on.

Best of all, in 1972 Morehouse College sponsored the world premiere of *Treemonisha* at the Atlanta Memorial Arts Center. Other productions soon followed, complete with scenery, costumes, and orchestra, and all the staging that Joplin had imagined. The opera opened on Broadway in September 1975 and received a Pulitzer Prize the following year.

W. C. HANDY

(1873–1958)

William Christopher Handy was born on Handy's Hill in Florence, Alabama, on November 16, 1873, in a log cabin with a dirt floor. His father was the Reverend Charles Handy, a stern Methodist preacher, and his mother was Elizabeth Handy.

As boys, William and his friends loved to make music using whatever was around. They made music on things like "fine-tooth combs," or by "drawing a broom handle across our first finger lying on a table" (to imitate a bass), and even by "scraping a twenty penny nail across the teeth" of a dead horse's "jawbone."[1] Yearning for a trumpet, William once tried to make a horn "by hollowing a cow horn and cutting the top into a mouthpiece."[2] By age ten, he could recognize and note on the musical scale almost any sound he heard—from riverboat whistles and laborers' songs and shouts on the nearby Tennessee River to the calls of hoot owls, cardinals, whippoorwills, and other birds. "Even the bellow of the bull became in my mind a musical note."[3]

Handy's grandmother, Thumuthis Handy, was the first to suggest that his "big ears" meant he had a talent for music. This announcement

thrilled the budding musician, "but I discovered almost immediately that life was not always a song."[4] His father was very strict about allowing only religious music in their home, and even visiting cousins were "forbidden to whistle."[5]

By working at odd jobs, W. C. saved up enough money to buy a guitar, but his father told him to return the guitar and exchange it for a dictionary. He was, however, allowed to take lessons on the organ so he could learn to play religious music. W. C.'s teacher was a noted Fisk University teacher, who gave the young musician the technical musical training he needed to write down the famous music he would later compose. Young Handy told his teacher that he wanted to be a musician. And the teacher told Handy's father, who wanted W. C. to be a minister like himself and his father before him, and therefore vigorously discouraged W. C. But the harsh words made him even more determined to pursue his dream.

After graduating with a teaching degree from Huntsville Teachers Agricultural and Mechanical College in Alabama in 1892, W. C. formed the Lauzette Quartet. They left Alabama and headed for Chicago, intending to play at the Chicago world's fair—only to find that the fair had been postponed until the next year. Penniless and jobless, they split up, and Handy went down to St. Louis, Missouri, which was a gathering place for ragtime musicians.

W. C.'s first break came in 1896 when a friend asked him to come to Chicago and play cornet in W. A. Mahara's Colored Minstrels for $6 a week. Pre–Civil War minstrel shows were comedy shows that featured white, mostly southern entertainers who blackened their faces, played the banjo, wore ragged, flashy clothing, and imitated African American singing, dancing, and speaking patterns. After the Civil War, minstrel shows became malicious because whites became much crueler in their caricatures of black people. Later, when black musicians were allowed to participate in the shows, they too had to blacken their faces.

What Are "the Blues"?

While in St. Louis, W. C. experienced exactly what "the blues" truly felt like. Handy was so poor that he had to sleep in vacant lots, in horses' stalls, and on the cold, wet levees of the Mississippi River. In poolhall chairs, he learned to sleep with his eyes open so that he wouldn't be thrown out as a sleeping vagrant. When Handy later wrote "St. Louis Blues," with the opening lines "I hate to see/de evenin' sun go down," he was writing about love relationships. But in the black community it also refers to being caught at night in a white man's town.

Many black performers moved up through the musical ranks and gained respect by performing in these shows. As bandleader and solo cornetist of the W. A. Mahara's Colored Minstrels, W. C. traveled around the country. In 1898, while in Kentucky, he met and married Elizabeth Price.

When the band went to Huntsville, Alabama, to perform, Handy's father went to hear them. After the show, a proud Reverend Handy told his son with a great handshake, "I am very proud of you and forgive you for becoming a musician."[6]

When Handy's wife became pregnant, he became head of the band, orchestra, and vocal music department at his Huntsville alma mater in September 1900. Unfortunately, the faculty felt that ragtime music, which Handy enjoyed, wasn't respectable. This conservative climate stifled Handy, and he returned to Mahara's Minstrels.

Handy's next major career move took him to Clarksdale, Mississippi, where he became the band director for the Black Knights of Pythias, and the orchestra they started later. While in Cleveland, Mississippi, Handy heard a different kind of blues from a foot-stomping, country string blues band that opened his eyes and his ears.

The audience was going wild. He began arranging his music to suit this foot-stomping beat.

> ✦**Arranging** means to adapt music especially for new voices, instruments, and styles of performance.

Handy continued to play and travel. He went to Memphis, which was another important stop on the Mississippi River music highway that roughly stretched from Chicago to New Orleans. Memphis would become the center of blues, rock and roll, and rhythm and blues, while its eastern sister Nashville would become the center of country music.

In 1909, Handy wrote a wordless campaign song for mayoral candidate Edward "Boss" Crump that he later called "Memphis Blues." This was the first blues song he had ever written. He published it in 1912, but was tricked into selling his copyright for $50 to a white publisher and songwriter. Today, Handy is recognized and credited as the creator of the "Memphis Blues," the first widely recognized blues song to be published.

Handy once said in an interview, "Each one of my blues is based on some old Negro song of the South. . . . Some old song that is a part of the memories of my childhood and of my race. I can tell you the exact song I used as a basis for any of my blues."[7]

While in Memphis, Handy also wrote and completed "St. Louis Blues" in September 1914. He followed this with "Beale Street Blues" and many others. At this time, sheet music was probably the most popular way of distributing and preserving music. He had thousands of copies of sheet music of his songs printed, and he sold them in department stores, music houses, and many other places nationwide. Soon, Handy and Harry Pace, a banker and a songwriter, became partners in Pace & Handy Music Company, Publishers.

In addition to writing, arranging, and publishing music, Handy also supervised a dozen bands, employed over sixty people, played at dances, and toured and gave concerts.

Unhappy with Memphis's continuing racism and riots, Handy and Pace moved their business to New York in 1918. Handy's staff increased into a "who's who" of musicians, including bandleader Fletcher Henderson and composer William Grant Still, who was second in charge of the arranging department.

As Handy worked to keep his struggling company going, he temporarily lost his sight. And as his health suffered, so did his financial situation. Although his eye problems and, later, a fall would cause him to become permanently blind, he courageously continued to work and build Handy Record Company, which he founded in 1922. In 1925, to help make financial ends meet, he edited *Blues: An Anthology,* a book about his work with blues music. This was one of the first books on African American popular music. His autobiography, *Father of the Blues: An Autobiography,* was published in 1941.

"I think America concedes that [true American music] has sprung from the Negro," Handy once said. "When we take these things that are our own, and develop them until they are finer things, that's pure culture. You've got to appreciate the things that come from the art of the Negro and from the heart of the man farthest down."[8]

He arranged and created blues pieces such as "Golden Brown Blues," with words by poet Langston Hughes; spirituals such as "In That Great Gettin' Up Morning," "Steal Away to Jesus," "Beale Street Serenade"; and *W. C. Handy's Collection of Negro Spirituals.*

W. C. Handy died of pneumonia on March 28, 1958, in New York City. At Handy's funeral, held at the Reverend Adam Clayton Powell's Abyssinian Baptist Church in Harlem, Powell said, "Gabriel now has an understudy and when the last trumpet shall sound, Handy will blow the last blues."[9]

That same year, a highly fictionalized film about Handy's life, *St. Louis Blues,* was released, starring singer Nat "King" Cole. Bessie Smith, who had recorded "St. Louis Blues" in 1925, also sang it in the movie.

W. C. Handy was inducted into the Nashville Songwriters Hall of Fame in 1983 and the Alabama Music Hall of Fame in 1987. Numerous festivals, including the W. C. Handy Music Festival and Music Camp in Florence, Alabama, are held in his honor. The W. C. Handy Blues Awards are held annually in Memphis, where his statue sits in Handy Park. His Beale Street home is a Memphis landmark.

THE BRASS BAND TRADITION

W. C. Handy, Louis Armstrong, and many other well-known musicians were either members or leaders of brass bands.

Brass bands, also called marching, military, and silver cornet bands, were prominent in small and moderate-size rural towns from around the 1870s through the 1930s. These "community" bands gave musicians the opportunity to hone their skills. Playing trumpets, cornets, trombones, clarinets, horns, and drums in a style that became the basis for early jazz, these bands had a repertoire that included marches, hymns, and spirituals. They performed in parades and at funerals (the famous "second line"), political stump rallies, fish fries, and other social functions

Though the popularity of brass bands has waned over time, a number of communities have retained the brass band tradition. The Old Morrisville Brass Band of Andrews, South Carolina, winners of a 1993 South Carolina Folk Heritage Award, has kept this tradition alive and well.

GERTRUDE "MA" RAINEY (PRIDGETT)

(1886–1939)

Called the Mother of the Blues, "Ma" Rainey was born Gertrude Pridgett on April 26, 1886, to Thomas and Ella Allen Pridgett. Her birthplace, Columbus, Georgia, was also the birthplace of musical prodigy Thomas "Blind Tom" Bethune. Her parents, and some say her grandmother, were in show business. Gertrude was only fourteen when she sang in her first revue, a talent show called A Bunch of Blackberries, at the Springer Opera House in Columbus.

While still in her teens, she went on the road with the minstrel tent shows and became a star. In 1904, at age eighteen, she married William "Pa" Rainey, a fellow performer. They called their song-and-dance team Rainey and Rainey, the Assassinators of the Blues. They toured with the Rabbit Foot Minstrel Shows, which she managed.

Ma Rainey was a sharp businesswoman who paid her entertainers on time and well. She and her jugglers, comedians, acrobats, and chorus girls performed "under a large circus tent with a portable wooden stage and Coleman lanterns for footlights."[1] The tent show traveled by train to southern and midwestern towns in time for their tobacco and

cotton harvests, and wintered in New Orleans. When her marriage broke up in 1917, Ma Rainey established her own company called Madam Gertrude Rainey and the Georgia Smart Set.

In the 1920s, her popular bluesy tunes caught the attention of Paramount music company. Their release of Ma Rainey's song "C. C. Rider," with trumpeter Louis Armstrong, established her as a recording star.

Ma Rainey was a great influence on many musicians of her time. Bessie Smith performed with her regularly. The founder of gospel, pianist Thomas Dorsey, traveled and recorded with Rainey in the 1920s when he was known as "Georgia Tom."

Ma Rainey was a short, heavy-set woman who loved to dress well—she wore necklaces made of gold coins, diamond earrings, furs, and sparkling, sequined dresses. "Her mouth was full of gold teeth, that sparkled in the spotlight."[2]

Whether she was dancing and singing at tent shows, in barns, in schoolhouses, or under the open sky, she was a favorite with black audiences. They connected with her sometimes naughty and humorous, sometimes sad, real-life songs such as "Gone Daddy Blues," "Screech Owl Blues," "Memphis Blues," "Walkin' the Dog," "Shave 'em Dry Blues," and "Prove It on Me Blues," which she wrote. Her

What Is the T.O.B.A.?

Ma Rainey was a headline star for the T.O.B.A.—the Theater Owners Booking Association. It was a talent agency that organized black musicians, singers, actors, and other entertainers to perform in selected towns around the country, usually in areas with large black populations. Schedules were tough, and in the segregated South and the prejudiced North, life was hard for the performers.

warm, generous, loving personality gained her the title of Ma. She often sponsored shows to benefit flood victims, the poor, and other people in need.

After the Great Depression in the 1930s, black vaudeville shows became practically extinct. Ma Rainey moved back home to Columbus, joined the Friendship Baptist Church, and managed two theaters in Columbus and Rome, Georgia. She died on December 22, 1939, of a heart attack, and is buried in Columbus. A plaque in her memory hangs at the Springer Opera House.

✦ **Vaudeville shows** were variety shows with short musical and comedy acts.

Ma Rainey, who wrote many of her own songs, has been called "a country woman to the core."[3] When she brought her down-home blues onto the stage, she became the best-known blues singer and songwriter of the 1920s. Music historian Chris Albertson wrote, "If there was another woman who sang the blues before Rainey, nobody remembered hearing her."[4] Rainey was inducted into the Rock and Roll Hall of Fame in 1990.

EUBIE BLAKE (1883–1983) NOBLE SISSLE (1889–1975)

The musicals created by the team of pianist and composer Eubie Blake and lyricist Noble Sissle helped transform American ragtime and helped launch the golden age of the Harlem Renaissance.

James Herbert "Eubie" Blake was born on February 7, 1883, in a four-room house at 319 Forest Street in Baltimore, Maryland. He was the only son of Emily Sumner Blake, a laundress, and John Sumner Blake, a stevedore crew chief. Both parents were former slaves. James was Emily and John Blake's only child of eleven children to survive infancy. Young James may have suffered from rickets, because he did not walk until he was three years old.

When Eubie was only four or five years old, he climbed up on a stool in a music store and began plunking on the organ. He received his first piano lessons from a neighbor, Mrs. Margaret Marshall, who gave him lessons even when his mother could not afford to pay her. Years later, when he was successful, he remembered his old music teacher's kindness and often visited her when he returned to Baltimore. He periodically repaid her generously for the quarters that his mother had not been able to afford.

BLAKE.

Remembering the hardships of slavery and the uncertainty of Reconstruction, John Sumner Blake often told his son that "a smart man never bites the hand that feeds him."[1] The Blakes were poor, hardworking, plain-speaking, loving parents. They were also very strict. They frowned on brass-band, honky-tonk, and ragtime music, which they considered bad influences. But at the time, this was America's popular music. Eubie loved it.

Noble Sissle, the other member of the team, was born in Indianapolis, Indiana, on July 10, 1889, into a middle-class religious family. His mother was a schoolteacher, and his father a minister. When Noble was a teenager, the family moved to Cleveland, Ohio, where he sang in his school's glee club and in a school quartet. After graduation, he became part of a vaudeville quartet that toured the Midwest.

✦ A **quartet** is a group of four performers.

In 1915, Sissle moved to Baltimore, where he met James Herbert Blake, who was already playing ragtime professionally. Blake had composed his first piano rag, "The Charleston Rag," in 1899. He had performed in Dr. Frazier's Medicine Show in 1901, and with the Old Kentucky stage show in 1902. He had married Avis Lee, a former schoolmate and a classical pianist, in 1910. Her father sang with the famous Black Patti Troubadours.

Noble and Eubie's first song written together was "It's All Your Fault" (1915), which the white singer Sophie Tucker used in her stage act. In 1916, just before the United States entered World War I, Sissle began working with James Reese Europe, the noted African American orchestra conductor and composer.

Sissle, Blake, and Europe became a curious trio. During the war, Sissle and Europe went to France to serve with the 369th Infantry Division of New York, and they recruited band members for Europe's 369th Infantry Band and wrote songs. Back in America, Eubie Blake put to music the lyrics his partners sent back to him. Tragically, the trio ended when James Reese Europe was murdered shortly after he returned from the war.

Blake and Sissle remained a team. They continued working in vaudeville shows until they met up with a black comedy team named Flournoy E. Miller and Aubrey Lyles. The four wrote the hit ragtime musical *Shuffle Along,* which opened in New York on May 23, 1921, to rave reviews.

Sissle and Blake followed this success with another musical, *Chocolate Dandies.* The duo toured Europe together in 1925, and then broke up to do separate tours. They teamed up again to write the 1933 sequel to *Shuffle Along.* Their last album together was *86 Years of Eubie Blake,* recorded in 1968–1969. Sissle died on December 17, 1975. They had been partners for over fifty years.

The energetic and prolific Eubie Blake continued creating and performing. Avis, his wife of twenty-nine years, died in 1939. He married Marion Tylor, a Los Angeles business executive and a performer, in 1945.

In his lifetime, Eubie Blake composed over 1,000 songs and musical pieces. He tried to retire in 1946, but ragtime, the beloved music of Scott Joplin, had a revival in the 1950s, 1960s, and 1970s. Eubie

The First Black Hit Musical Show

Shuffle Along was the first successful all-black musical of its time. Composer William Grant Still, choir director Hall Johnson, dancer Florence Mills, singer and dancer Josephine Baker, and concert singer Paul Robeson were among the many black musicians and performers who worked on the show and went on to build legendary careers.

Two of the more enduring songs from the musical were the wildly popular "I'm Just Wild About Harry" and "Love Will Find a Way."

Blake, the last of the ragtime celebrities, suddenly found himself surrounded by an admiring and attentive international audience. He had become a national treasure and the elder statesman for ragtime music.

JAMES REESE EUROPE

James Reese Europe (1881–1919) was one of the country's most talented and innovative African American musicians in his day. He organized the Clef Club Symphony Orchestra and the Clef Club, one of the country's first large unions of black musicians. While serving in France during World War I, James Reese Europe created the 369th Infantry Band, whose music dazzled French audiences. He is considered by many to be the first musician who "took jazz abroad and made a lasting impression."[2]

James Reese Europe with the Clef Club Orchestra, which he organized.

Over the years, Eubie Blake received many awards, including the James P. Johnson Award in 1970 and the Duke Ellington Medal in 1972. He was featured in the 1976 Broadway show *Eubie,* and made many television appearances around the world. Presidents also found favor with his music. President Harry S. Truman's 1948 campaign song was Sissle and Blake's "I'm Just Wild about Harry." Eubie Blake received the Presidential Medal of Honor in 1981.

Eubie Blake died on February 12, 1983, in Brooklyn, New York, at the incredible age of 100. He was honored on a U.S. postal stamp as a jazz composer and pianist.

Francis Hall JOHNSON

(1888–1970)

Combining classical training with his memories of old slave songs heard during his childhood, composer and choir director Francis Hall Johnson published authentic arrangements of the old spirituals. Choirs and concert singers still perform his music today.

From the moment Hall, as he was known, was born on March 12, 1888, in Athens, Georgia, he was hearing and internalizing the black spirituals, praise, and sorrow songs sung by his family and neighbors. Since many of them were former slaves, they sang with the passion of authenticity.

Hall's grandmother was enslaved until she was thirty, and she usually "sang or hummed at her work all day long; and it is largely because of the childhood years of listening to her" and others that spirituals became "as natural" to him "as breathing."[1] Johnson himself has said that "the memory of those old-time singers and the songs they created became the most powerful single influence upon my life."[2]

His mother, enslaved until she was eight, was an accomplished singer who attended Atlanta University. His father, an African

Hall Johnson (rear, right) *and his siblings stand behind their parents. Young Hall could always find a source of creativity and inspiration in his family.*

Methodist Episcopal minister named William Decker Johnson, was a freedman. Hall, one of five children, began playing the piano with the help of an older sister. By age eight, Hall "was already jotting down tunes," and even saw concert singer Sissieretta Jones (also known as Black Patti) perform during her visits to Athens, Georgia.[3]

Seeing violinist Joseph Douglass perform so inspired Hall that he set out to learn to play the violin. He started by teaching himself from a booklet he purchased at a ten-cent store, and his father also gave him lessons.

When Hall turned sixteen, his father became president of Allen University in Columbia, South Carolina. Hall also attended Allen but moved on to Atlanta University and other schools in his search for a good musical education. Eager to find professional violin instruction but unable to find it in the South, Johnson moved to Philadelphia, where he attended the Hahn School of Music at the University of Pennsylvania. He graduated with a Certificate in Music in 1910.

That same year, he gave his first professional violin concert in New York. By 1914, he was living in New York, where he opened a violin studio and also continued his studies at the prestigious Juilliard School of Music.

Because of Johnson's expertise on the violin and the viola, he got jobs with composer James Reese Europe's orchestra and Will Marion Cook's New York Syncopated Orchestra. He also played in the Lyle and Miller pit orchestra for musicals. One of those musicals was Noble Sissle and Eubie Blake's 1921 successful all-black *Shuffle Along.*

Johnson decided to organize a professional choir. He wanted his choir to perform these spirituals just as they would have been performed in the old days.

On September 8, 1925, Johnson formed his eight-person choir. At first, they were called the Harlem Jubilee Singers, but the choir gradually grew to thirty people and became known as the Hall Johnson Choir. The choir had its first formal performance in New York on February 26, 1926. Most members were originally from the South and were already familiar with the style of music Johnson wanted to create.

In 1930, Johnson wrote and arranged the music for Marc Connolly's Pulitzer Prize–winning play *The Green Pastures.* The Hall Johnson Choir performed in the play. Reviewers wrote that without the spirited singing of the choir, the play would not have been so popular.

Johnson next wrote a book and a play called *Run Little Chillun,* named after the old spiritual. The play opened on Broadway in 1933 and had a successful four-month run. The movie version of *Green Pastures* was made in 1935, and about a year later, Johnson received an honorary doctorate in music from the Philadelphia Music Academy.

The original Fisk Jubilee Singers. The choral tradition begun by the Fisk Jubilee Singers is very much alive today.

The Fisk Jubilee Singers— The Choral Tradition

The Hall Johnson Choir was part of a great tradition of African American choral music. The Fisk Jubilee Singers, for example, began in 1866 as a group of Fisk University students who sang Negro folk songs, popular melodies, and some spirituals. In 1871, the school-sponsored group, many of whom were former slaves, started touring America and Europe to raise money for their school. They thus introduced to the world the beauty and magnificence of what writer Gwendolin Sims Warren calls "arranged spirituals."

From 1875 to 1978, the singers traveled to Europe again, performing before royalty. They eventually earned more than $150,000 for their school. Since that time, all the Fisk Jubilee groups and quartets have traveled about the country and the world, singing spirituals and popular songs.

Under his directorship, the choir sang in the films *Lost Horizon* (1937), *Way Down South* (1939), and *Cabin in the Sky* (1943). They also made several successful recordings.

Johnson continued to create new arrangements of traditional spirituals, such as "Swing Low, Sweet Chariot" and "There Is a Balm in Gilead." In his book *Thirty Negro Spirituals,* he included instructions on how they should be sung, played, and presented.

For a while, Johnson lived in California and organized choirs. But he returned to New York in 1946 and organized the Festival Negro Chorus of New York City. The Hall Johnson Choir continued to perform with distinction. In 1951, at the request of the U.S. Department of State, the Hall Johnson Choir participated in the International Festival of Fine Arts in Berlin, Germany, and went on to tour Europe.

Johnson received numerous awards for his contribution to music, including the Simon Haessler Prize from the University of Pennsylvania in 1910, the Holstein Prize in 1927, the Harmon Award in 1930, and the City of New York's Handel Award. Later in life, he also taught great singers such as classical soprano Shirley Verrett.

Hall Johnson once said, "One hundred years from now people may not even be able to conceive of what slavery was like except through books, but if we keep the music alive they will know 'Swing Low Sweet Chariot' generations from now."[4]

Johnson died on April 30, 1970, from injuries he received in a fire at his apartment in New York.

BESSIE SMITH

(1894–1937)

Bessie Smith, known as the Empress of the Blues, was born in stunning poverty on April 15, 1894, in Chattanooga, Tennessee. Good-paying jobs for African Americans in the South at the turn of the century weren't easy to find. Her father, William Smith, was a part-time Baptist preacher; her mother, Laura Smith, was a laundress. The family lived in a one-room shack. Bessie was one of several children, and by the time she turned nine, both parents had died. She had a right to sing the blues.

Bessie and her siblings grew up largely without adult supervision and protection. They learned early in life to be resourceful, both in protecting themselves from the harsh life of the streets and in providing for themselves. With her older brothers Clarence and Andrew, young Bessie often danced and sang for pennies on Chattanooga's dusty streets.

Influenced by the popularity and growing respect that traveling black vaudeville show musicians enjoyed, Bessie dreamed of singing

and dancing professionally. She did, however, manage to attend school long enough to learn to read and write.

One of Bessie's passions was roller-skating. When she was eight years old, she started entering and winning amateur skating contests. She saved enough money from her winnings to rent and then buy a pair of ball-bearing roller skates. Bessie Smith went on to win the Tennessee roller-skating championship in Chattanooga.[1]

When her brother Clarence joined the Moses Stokes traveling vaudeville show, Bessie was thrilled. She soon joined him, and in 1912 began her professional career. Legends abound as to how Bessie came to work with Gertrude Pridgett, known as "Ma" Rainey, the pioneering singer called the Mother of the Blues. According to one version, Ma Rainey took to the sassy young singer so much that she ordered two of her workers to kidnap Bessie. They brought a fuming and fighting Bessie to Rainey's trailer in a burlap sack. The two women, of course, hit it off.

Bessie Smith toured with Ma Rainey in Fat Chappelle's Rabbit Foot Minstrels tent show through the South in 1915. They remained good friends throughout their lives and even wrote a few songs together. Audiences loved Bessie Smith, Ma Rainey's teenage protégée.

✦ A **protégée** is a young female performer who is being trained by a master. A **protégé** is a young male performer.

✦ A **contralto** voice is a rare, low woman's singing voice.

Bessie traveled around the South with other minstrel shows, gaining fans everywhere. Her impressive resonant contralto voice thrilled her devoted fans, and by the time she reached her early twenties, her smooth, sultry voice would become the standard for "professional blues" around the world

By 1920, she was producing her own shows for the 81 Theater in Atlanta and taking them on the road. Eager to record her music, Bessie had to try five times (producers said her voice was "too rough") before getting a record contract. In 1923, Columbia Records released her first recording, "Down-Hearted Blues." It sold nearly a million records in its first year.

In all, Bessie sang and recorded about 160 songs and wrote more than 25. She recorded such blues classics as "Tain't Nobody's Bizness If I Do," "Back Water Blues," "Poor Man's Blues," and "St. Louis Blues." She also worked with Louis Armstrong and Benny Goodman.

The woman from the hills of Chattanooga never strayed far from her street roots. She maintained an acute awareness of herself as an African American woman, and she continually fought to keep control over her music and her career. One time, when theater owners said that the chorus girls in her Liberty Belles traveling show were too plump and too dark-skinned, she replied that if they didn't work, she wouldn't, either.

Bessie was married to law enforcement officer Jack Gee for a short time, but they divorced. She maintained a financially comfortable lifestyle, and unlike many other blues musicians who lost work during the Great Depression, she stayed active. Smith continued to headline at New York's famed Apollo Theater, starred in a Philadelphia nightclub show, knocked audiences dead at tent shows and cabarets (mostly in her beloved South), and even performed with a swing band. Bessie Smith was the country's highest-paid black entertainer of her day. Wherever she went, "her appearances caused serious traffic jams around theaters from Detroit to New Orleans."[2]

While working in a traveling show in the South called "Broadway Rastus," she suffered massive injuries in an automobile accident near Clarksdale, Mississippi. She died September 26, 1937, at G. T. Thomas Hospital, an African American hospital in Clarksdale.

Bessie Smith, the Empress of the Blues, influenced gospel composer Thomas Dorsey and his music. Many other musicians, including gospel singer Mahalia Jackson, jazz great Billie Holiday, and white rock singer Janis Joplin admired her style, as do many musicians today.

Bessie Smith is buried in Mount Lawn Cemetery in Sharon Hill,

Pennsylvania. She was inducted into the Blues Foundation's Hall of Fame in 1980, the National Women's Hall of Fame in 1984, and the Rock and Roll Hall of Fame in 1989.

BESSIE AND THE MOVIES

In 1929, Bessie Smith starred in her own seventeen-minute, two-reel movie. In it, she sings "St. Louis Blues," the W. C. Handy classic, accompanied by the Fletcher Henderson Band and the Hall Johnson Choir. The film clip was later included in the 1958 movie version of *St. Louis Blues,* a highly fictionalized version of blues composer W. C. Handy's life, starring Nat "King" Cole. Also appearing in the movie were Pearl Bailey, Mahalia Jackson, Ella Fitzgerald, Ruby Dee, and Eartha Kitt.

MARIAN ANDERSON

(1897–1993)

Marian Anderson was born February 27, 1897, on Webster Street in Philadelphia. She was the oldest of three daughters born to John and Anna Anderson. John Anderson, an officer of Union Baptist Church, worked at the Reading Terminal Market and sold ice and coal to earn extra money. Anna Anderson, a quiet, dignified woman, had been a schoolteacher in Virginia. Because she could not get a license to teach in Philadelphia, she took in washing to help make ends meet.

By the time Marian was six years old, she was singing in Union Baptist's Junior Choir. When she was eight, she gave her first "concert" at a church program, where she was described as "the ten-year-old contralto."[1] Marian loved music so much that she would pretend that the flowers on the wallpaper in her home were people, and would sing to them.

Marian scrubbed her neighbors' porch steps in their South Philadelphia community to earn enough nickels and dimes to buy a $3.45 violin from a nearby pawnshop. She played it "until the strings gave way."[2] After the violin fell apart, Marian persuaded her father

to buy a piano. She and her sisters, Alyse and Ethel, taught themselves to play piano by using a keyboard note guide.

When Marian was eight years old, tragedy visited the close-knit family: her father suffered a fatal injury at work and died at Christmastime. After Mr. Anderson's death, Anna Anderson and the girls moved in with his parents. Anna Anderson worked long hours and guided her daughters "by her example."

Marian was profoundly affected by her mother's quiet strength. She learned at an early age to look at life with a very direct view of what was right, what was wrong, what was appropriate and what was not, and to be conscientious of other people's peace and quiet. Marian helped her mother as much as she could, but she longed for the day when her mother would not have to work so hard and when they could have their own home again.

By age thirteen she was singing with the Union Baptist Church Senior Choir and substituting for absent choir members. She was active in the Baptist Young People's Union, and even though she was only a teenager, the church often sent her to represent its choirs and quartets at other churches as far away as New York. She remained in the church's choirs until she was almost twenty-one and never missed a Sunday. Marian explained, "The congregation made me feel that I was an indispensable part of what went on there."[3]

Marian went to William Penn High School, where she joined the chorus. She also wanted to acquire office skills so that she could get a job and help her family. The teen was encouraged to pursue a more formal music education, and she transferred to South Philadelphia High School for Girls. She continued singing at churches and social functions, earning up to $5 per engagement. Marian always used her earnings to help with the family finances. She graduated from South Philadelphia High in 1921.

Marian received her first real vocal lessons from Mrs. Mary Saunders Patterson, a black soprano who coached her for free.

Marian's church also sponsored a fund-raising concert that allowed her to study with the famous voice teacher Giuseppe Boghetti.

She started entering competitions, and winning them, while still doing performances to earn money. When she had saved enough, she purchased a house for her mother.

In 1924, Marian gave a concert at New York's Town Hall. Because she had very little experience singing in German, she did not perform the German songs very well. Her performance was harshly criticized. She returned to Philadelphia discouraged and disappointed with her performance.

Marian eventually regained her confidence and resumed her voice lessons with Boghetti. In 1925, she competed with over 300 contestants in the National Music League auditions and won first prize, even though she was suffering from an abscessed ear. She had also started appearing at Carnegie Hall as a soloist with the Hall Johnson Choir and was receiving excellent reviews.

Still determined to improve her singing of German *lieder,* she traveled to Germany, where she learned to sing them properly. In 1930, she sponsored her own concert and made a triumphant debut in Berlin, Germany.

✦ **Lieder** is the German word for songs.

Europeans quickly accepted this talented black singer. "Even the first curiosity about my outward difference was in no way disturbing or offensive, and it seemed only a moment before that dropped away," recalled Ms. Anderson.[4]

Marian Anderson sang in the United States in December 1935 at the same New York Town Hall where she had sung poorly over a decade earlier. This time she sang perfectly. She ended the concert triumphantly with a selection of spirituals she had been singing since childhood.

She returned to Europe, where she continued to receive appreciation and acclaim for her performances. Traveling on trains, in chauffeured automobiles, and in small planes through storms and fog across

Europe, the African American lady from Philadelphia stood on Swedish, Danish, Italian, German, Russian, and French stages, singing with her eyes closed and a picture of the audience in her mind. She became so popular that one European newspaper called the public's adoration of her "Marian Fever."

In 1942, after a long relationship, Marian Anderson married her teenage sweetheart, architect Orpheus H. "King" Fisher. They moved to

A Glorious Concert

On Easter Sunday, April 9, 1939, 75,000 people came by car, bus, train, plane, and on foot to hear Marian Anderson's magnificent voice and to show their support. She sang from the steps of the Lincoln Memorial in Washington, D.C. Here's how the concert came about:

Howard University's School of Music in Washington, D.C., had asked Marian Anderson to perform in its annual concert series, which she had participated in for several years. When a fire destroyed their theater, the university had to find someplace else to hold the event. First, they asked permission to use the nearby, whites-only Central High School auditorium, but their request was refused because of the city's policy of racial segregation. Then Howard University asked the Daughters of the American Revolution (DAR) for permission to use its prestigious Constitution Hall. The DAR said no, also because of racial segregation.

Mrs. Eleanor Roosevelt, wife of President Franklin Roosevelt and a DAR member, publicly resigned from the group in protest. With Mrs. Roosevelt's encouragement, Harold L. Ickes, U.S. secretary of the interior, invited Ms. Anderson and the Howard University Choir to give a free concert at the Lincoln Memorial. The situation brought to Marian Anderson's mind the Philadelphia music school's refusal to even give her admission papers when as a teenager she had tried to enroll. She thought of the many times whites refused to allow her to eat or sleep at segregated American hotels, and the times when she had to ride in segregated trains and sing to segregated audiences. But she agreed to appear at the Lincoln Memorial. Whether she liked it or not, she had become "a symbol, representing my people. I *had* to appear."[5]

a farm in Danbury, Connecticut. Marian Anderson loved animals. On their Connecticut farm, she and her husband kept several animals, including horses, a cat named Snoopy, and a spoiled puppy who chewed up a blue velvet handbag belonging to one of their guests. She even recorded an album called *Snoopy Cat: The Adventures of Marian Anderson's Cat, Snoopy.*

Anderson had no children but was very close to her nephew, James DePreist, who later became a symphony conductor.

On January 7, 1955, Marian Anderson broke another racial barrier. She became the first African American to sing with the Metropolitan Opera as Ulrica in *Un Ballo in Maschera,* an opera by Giuseppe Verdi. She continued performing, singing for the armed forces around the world, and eventually singing at Constitution Hall.

She received honorary degrees from universities world wide, and won prestigious awards for her music and her spirit. Among her awards were the $10,000 Bok Prize given to Philadelphia residents for outstanding service, the NAACP's Spingarn Award, and the Presidential Medal of Freedom presented to her by President Lyndon Johnson in 1963.

In 1957–1958, she served as a Goodwill Ambassador for the U.S. State Department, and sang for the presidential inaugurations of both Dwight Eisenhower and John F. Kennedy.

In 1939, Marian Anderson performed in the Easter Sunday concert held at the Lincoln Memorial in Washington, D.C.

She retired in 1965, but continued to be active in musical activities and remained at her farm until after her husband's death. In July 1992, she moved to her nephew's home in Portland, Oregon. She suffered a stroke in early 1993 and died of congestive heart failure at home on April 8, 1993.

Roland Hayes—An Inspiring Mentor

Marian Anderson's musical inspiration was the distinguished international tenor Roland Hayes. Every year, he gave concerts at her church, and he recommended her to many people.

Roland Hayes was born in Curryville, Georgia, on June 3, 1887, on the same plantation where his mother had been enslaved. After his father's death when Roland was a child, he moved to Chattanooga, Tennessee. He sang in the New Monumental Baptist Church Choir on Eighth Street. While he was a music student at Fisk University in Nashville, Tennessee, he sang with the Fisk Jubilee Singers.

When the group traveled to Boston in 1911, Hayes remained behind. He took voice lessons and supported himself through odd jobs. Though Hayes received no encouragement to be a classical singer, he persevered. His first recital was on November 15, 1917. Hayes traveled to Europe in 1920–1921, where he gave a command performance for King George V in England.

In 1923, he made his Carnegie Hall debut. He also sang with the Boston Symphony. He was the first African American to appear with a major international orchestra. Roland Hayes was an outstanding interpreter of spirituals as well as the classics. He was a member of the music faculty at Boston University, and the University of Tennessee at Chattanooga named its fine arts center after him.

A recipient of many honorary degrees, including the prestigious NAACP's Spingarn Medal for "most outstanding achievement among colored people," Hayes was a mentor for many aspiring African American classical singers. He died on January 1, 1977.

PAUL ROBESON

(1898–1976)

Paul Robeson was born on April 9, 1898, in Princeton, New Jersey. Destined for a life on concert stages around the world, Robeson was the youngest child of the Reverend William and Maria Bustill Robeson. Both came from freedom-loving, strong black families.

Paul's father had been a slave. At age fifteen, William Robeson ran away from a Raleigh, North Carolina, area plantation and joined the Union army. He learned to read and write, moved to Princeton, New Jersey, and married. Maria Robeson, a schoolteacher who came from a family of Quakers and abolitionists, died when Paul was a child.

Young Paul adored his father and admired the "rock-like strength and dignity of his character."[1] Through his father's example, Paul learned to be loyal to his convictions, no matter what. In his father's church, he also learned the old Negro spirituals and hymns.

Paul grew up to be a stunning 6 feet 3 inches tall. He went to Rutgers University, where he excelled in his studies and was an All-American football player. As valedictorian of his class, Robeson spoke on equality for black people at his graduation in 1919. Paul entered

Columbia Law School the following year, and in 1921 married an equally strong willed woman named Eslanda Cardozo Goode, a descendant of Francis Cardozo, a former enslaved man who became an educator and South Carolina secretary of state.

Eslanda Robeson encouraged Paul's talent as a performer. At her suggestion, he took the part of Simon, Jesus Christ's cross bearer, in a Harlem YMCA production of *Simon, the Cyrenian* in 1920. This brought his talents to the attention of playwright Eugene O'Neill.

Robeson graduated from Columbia Law School in 1923. While working at a law firm, he became furious when a white secretary there refused to take dictation from him. He quit the firm and never practiced law again.

Encouraged by favorable responses to his performance in a number of productions, Paul accepted the leading roles in Eugene O'Neill's plays *All God's Chillun Got Wings* and *The Emperor Jones* in 1924. The next year, he teamed up with pianist Lawrence Brown and performed the first solo concert of African American spirituals on stage in New York. The concert launched his singing career. He gave concerts abroad, and made his first album. He returned to New York and played the character Crown in the 1928 musical play *Porgy*. He also played the role of Jim in Jerome Kern's *Show Boat* in London.

Robeson's compelling performance of the song "Ol' Man River" in *Show Boat* was so memorable that it became one of his signature songs, along with "Deep River," by black songwriter Harry T. Burleigh. Robeson's favorite role, and the one he is most remembered for, was the Moor in Shakespeare's *Othello,* which he first performed in London in 1930.

Robeson, who was fluent in nine languages, made over 300 recordings. He also appeared in numerous movies. His first was Oscar Micheaux's *Body and Soul,* then the film versions of *The Emperor Jones, King Solomon's Mines,* and *Showboat.*

Throughout his many successes, Paul Robeson constantly fought against racism. He spoke out publicly against lynchings, segregation, poor housing, economic injustice, police brutality, other racist woes, and fascism. He approved of liberation for colonized African countries, and supported labor unions during the anti-union years of the 1930s.

Because of his outspoken beliefs, the United States government believed he was a member of the Communist Party. In 1941, the FBI began watching him. In 1943, they declared that he was a leading Communist. That same year, he became the first African American to play the role of Othello on Broadway with a white cast.

Despite the government's harassment, Robeson continued to hold fast to his beliefs, just as he had learned from his father. He later wrote in his autobiography, *Here I Stand,* "I saw no reason why my convictions should change with the weather. I was not raised that way, and neither the promise of gain nor the threat of loss has ever moved me from my firm convictions."[2]

Robeson's career suffered because he spoke out against injustice when he saw it. During a World Peace Congress in Paris in 1949, he said, "It is unthinkable that American Negroes will go to war on behalf of those who have oppressed us for generations against a country [the Soviet Union] which in one generation has raised our people to the full dignity of mankind."[3]

Cities and towns across the United States and veterans groups refused to let him sing in their halls. He nearly lost his life in Peekskill, New York, when a riot broke out during his concert. By 1951, in the midst of the Cold War between the United States and the Soviet Union, the U.S. government, the NAACP's Roy Wilkins, many other prominent African Americans, and even American television networks denounced Robeson for his views. The criticisms increased when he received a $25,000 Stalin Peace Prize from the Soviet Union in 1952. It was just one of many tributes and awards he received throughout his life, including the NAACP's prestigious Spingarn Award.

Robeson as the Moor in Shakespeare's Othello, *his favorite and most memorable role.*

But even though his passport was revoked in 1950 and his travel abroad was restricted, and despite having his life threatened and being repeatedly called to renounce communism before the U.S. House Committee on Un-American Activities, Robeson sang wherever he could. He continued speaking out against racial and economic injustice. When record companies refused to record him, Robeson and his son, Paul Jr., founded Othello Recording Company and recorded the albums *Paul Robeson Sings* and *Solid Rock.* From time to time, he even sang by telephone to assembled audiences in England and Wales.

Like his iron-willed father, Robeson remained unbossed and unbowed to the end. In 1958, he regained his passport as a result of a related U.S. Supreme Court ruling. After the court victory, Robeson sang to a sold-out crowd at Carnegie Hall, published his autobiography, and once again began singing and touring around the world. After Eslanda Robeson's death in 1965, Robeson settled in Philadelphia with his sister, Mrs. Marian Forsythe. On his seventy-fifth birthday, he was honored and his work celebrated at Carnegie Hall. He died on January 23, 1976, in Philadelphia.

In 1998, on the one-hundredth anniversary of his birth, fans and historians around the world celebrated his achievements. He also received posthumously a Grammy Lifetime Achievement Award.

Simon Estes—Lending a Hand

Like Paul Robeson, bass baritone opera singer Simon Estes did not set out to make a career in the world of music. Simon was born in Centerville, Iowa, on February 2, 1938. He was the son of Simon Estes, a coal miner, and Ruth Estes. Young Simon sang in the Second Baptist Church and in high school choirs. While studying pre-med and psychology at the University of Iowa, he became the first black member of the university's Old Gold Singers. His music teacher encouraged him to study opera, and in 1963 Estes won a full scholarship to attend the Juilliard School of Music in New York. Since then, he has become known throughout the world for his opera, concert, and recital performances.

Once, while singing in the Cape Town, South Africa, Opera Festival, he saw such debilitating poverty that he adopted a public high school. It's now called Simon Estes Music High School. He also established the Simon Estes International Foundation for Children, which helps assist underprivileged children with their educational and health needs.

DUKE ELLINGTON

(1899–1974)

Nearly all major American jazz, blues, and big band instrumentalists and singers have either performed with composer, musician, and bandleader "Duke" Ellington or sung his songs. A handsome, romantic, passionate, talented, and prolific renaissance man, Ellington wrote over 2,000 compositions. Many are classics today.

Edward Kennedy Ellington was born into a warm and well-established, piano-playing, middle-class family on April 29, 1899, in Washington, D.C. His mother was Daisy Kennedy Ellington, and his father was James Edward Ellington, a butler and caterer. Ellington loved and respected his parents, and when his beloved sister, Ruth, was born sixteen years later, she immediately became the baby doll of the family.

When he was six, Edward began taking piano lessons with a teacher named Mrs. Clinkscales, but he preferred playing baseball. He loved the sport so much that one of his first jobs was to yell, "Peanuts, popcorn, chewing gum, candy, cigars, cigarettes, and score cards!" to the crowds at a Washington baseball park.[1]

Several years later, after watching a young kid play the piano in Philadelphia, Ellington began fiddling with the piano again. He later wrote, "I hadn't been able to get off the ground before, but after hearing him, I said to myself, 'Man, you're just going to *have* to do it.'"[2] Inspired by the young man's playing, he composed his first song, "Soda Fountain Rag," in memory of his job as a soda jerk as a teenager at the Poodle Dog Café.

It was around this time that Ellington received the nickname Duke. He explained that a popular, well-dressed friend named Edgar McEntree gave him the nickname just before he entered high school. Ellington later became known for his elegant manner and for being a snappy dresser, which he said that Washingtonians were known for, anyway. This may be where the expression "being duked out"—that is, being well-dressed, wearing trendy clothes—came from. Over the years, Ellington gained a number of other nicknames from friends: Otto, because he had been such a good second baseman; Dump, which was short for apple dumpling; Puddin; and Head Knocker.

Like many other adventurous young men in the early days of ragtime, jazz, and blues music, Ellington and his buddies would slip into neighborhood cabarets, dances, theaters, and pool rooms (now called billiard parlors), where he heard, saw, and was influenced by such talented piano players as Doc Perry, James P. Johnson, and Louis Brown. Perry, who heard Ellington play, became one of the teenager's mentors.

Ellington, who was also a talented painter, was earning money playing the piano by the time he was eighteen. Although he had turned down an art scholarship after graduating from high school so he could pursue his music, he used his expertise to paint signs and earn extra income. While playing piano in Washington, D.C., he met and became friends with many musicians, including bandleader Fletcher Henderson. Ellington dreamed of putting together a big band just like Henderson's.

On July 2, 1918, he married Edna Thompson, and they had a son named Mercer. Duke organized a small band the following year. In 1923, he moved to New York City, where he formed a larger band called the Washingtonians, with other D.C. musicians.

Ellington arrived in New York when the Harlem Renaissance was at its height. Pianists Willie the Lion Smith and Fats Waller, pianist and bandleader Count Basie, violinist and composer Will Marion Cook, and sax and clarinet player Sidney Bechet were among the many musicians who became friends with Ellington.

The young composer recorded his first song, "Choo Choo," in 1924. His big break arrived in 1927 when he and his band accepted an offer to play at Harlem's famous show club, the whites-only Cotton Club. Owned by whites, the Cotton Club featured high-powered, flashy music revues with scantily clad black female dancers and singers. Ellington's music was broadcast live over the radio. In 1931, Ellington and his orchestra left the club.

Ellington always wrote music wherever he was, and at all times of the day and night. He took everything he heard around him—trains, street and alley sounds, animal cries—and put it into his music. Then it was up to his orchestra to give sound to his arrangements. Trumpeters Charles "Cootie" Williams and Cat Anderson, alto sax player Johnny Hodges, and all the other musicians in the Duke Ellington Orchestra brought the Duke's music to life.

In 1933, the band made its first trip to Europe, where it received a warm welcome. This was the first of its many tours abroad. During this time, Ellington wrote popular songs like "Mood Indigo," "It Don't Mean a Thing If It Ain't Got That Swing," "Sophisticated Lady," "Solitude," and "Echoes of Harlem."

Ellington's orchestra became even more popular when arranger, pianist, and songwriter Billy "Sweet Pea" Strayhorn joined it in 1939. Ellington said that Strayhorn became "my right arm, my left arm, all the eyes in the back of my head, my brain waves in his head, and his in mine."[3] Strayhorn wrote the orchestra's theme song, "Take the A

Here Duke Ellington and his famous orchestra take pleasure in playing together.

Train," in 1941. He and Ellington wrote many songs together. They adapted Tchaikovsky's Nutcracker Suite; they created the Liberian Suite, the musical *Jump for Joy,* and *Black, Brown and Beige,* a history of the Negro in music that premiered at Carnegie Hall. They even honored Shakespeare with a song called "Such Sweet Thunder." Strayhorn died in 1967.

"Ellington's ability to change musical styles and his constant experimentation" were important to his continued success "as one of the major music makers of the twentieth century."[4] A deeply religious man, he turned in later years to creating religious music and jazz concerts, which he performed in churches here and abroad. His signature good-bye song after a performance was "We Love You Madly." Ellington has summarized his career by saying, "I live a life . . . with the mind of a child and an unquenchable thirst for sharps and flats."

He also said, "Music is my mistress, and she plays second fiddle to no one."[5]

During Ellington's career, this black star and his wonderful orchestra performed before heads of state around the world, appeared in movies, and recorded with top jazz artists such as Ella Fitzgerald, Louis Armstrong, John Coltrane, Coleman Hawkins, Frank Sinatra, Tony Bennett, and Sarah Vaughan.

The band won every major musical award. They received *Down Beat, Esquire,* and *Playboy* magazines' top awards and the Jazz Critics Poll's highest rankings. They also won a number of Grammy Awards, and the musical score Ellington wrote for the motion picture *Paris Blues* was nominated for an Oscar.

✦ A **musical score** is the music written for a movie or stage show.

In 1959, he received the NAACP's prestigious Spingarn Medal. In 1969, during Ellington's seventieth birthday celebration at the White House, President Richard Nixon presented him with the Presidential Medal of Freedom. Sixteen American colleges and universities presented him with honorary degrees. Cities around the United States honored him with keys to their cities. The African countries of Chad and Togo issued Ellington postage stamps, as did the United States in 1986; and he was made an honorary citizen of Niigata, Japan.

Local, national, and international music organizations, including the Royal Swedish Academy of Music, groups of all kinds, churches, fraternities, and sororities have all honored the Duke in some way. Pope Paul VI gave him a special papal blessing in 1969, and many Duke Ellington Societies thrive around the world today.

Duke Ellington died of cancer and pneumonia at Columbia Presbyterian Medical Center's Harkness Pavilion in New York on May 24, 1974. He had been actively composing music until shortly before the end. His son, Mercer, continued the Ellington Orchestra until his death in 1996. Duke Ellington's youngest grandson, Paul, leads the Duke Ellington Orchestra today. His granddaughter, Mercedes Ellington, is president of the Duke Ellington Foundation that continues to honor her grandfather's artistic and literary talents.

In 1999, twenty-five years after his death, Duke Ellington was awarded the Pulitzer Prize in music.

Essentially Ellington

Essentially Ellington is a national educational program. It is an annual high school jazz band competition offered by Jazz at Lincoln Center in New York, and is led by renowned trumpeter and Jazz at Lincoln Center Artistic Director Wynton Marsalis. Each year, interested schools receive original Ellington arrangements, then participate in school workshops to learn how to perform the composer's music. Finalists compete at the three-day festival, which is traditionally held around Ellington's birthday. Established in 1996, the competition is now open to schools in all fifty states and the U.S. territories.

THOMAS ANDREW DORSEY

(1899–1993)

When slave songs, spirituals, work songs and chanties, ragtime, and blues came together during the 1920s in composer-pianist Thomas Andrew Dorsey's compositions, he called it "gospel music," a "blend of sacred texts and blues tunes."[1] Many churchgoers who had migrated to the North from the southern fields, and the families and loves they had left behind, embraced this new spiritual musical expression because it reminded them of a musical "letter from home."[2]

Thomas Dorsey's gospel songs "Precious Lord, Take My Hand," "Walk All Over God's Heaven," and "There'll Be Peace in the Valley" have been sung, recorded, and loved by millions of people around the world.

Thomas Andrew Dorsey was born July 1, 1899, to the Reverend Thomas M. and Etta Dorsey in Villa Rica, Georgia, a country town located not far from Atlanta. He was born into a musical family—his mother played the church organ, an uncle was a choir director, and another was a guitarist. His father was a schoolteacher and minister. Young Thomas liked to play on the family organ whenever he got the chance.

In church, the spirituals were often accompanied by what Thomas thought of as "moanin'." This was a wordless, heartfelt musical humming of a song rather than actual singing of the words. "That kind of singing would stir the churches up more so than one of those fast hymns,"[3] Dorsey recalled. "They'd get more shouts out of the moans than they did sometimes out of the words."[4] Memories of that heartfelt expression rising from those black Baptist southern country churches where his father preached made a lifelong impression on Thomas.

In search of a better life, the family moved to Atlanta while Thomas was still a youngster. But even in Atlanta, the family remained poor. Much to Thomas's acute embarrassment, children laughed at his worn clothes and ridiculed his dark skin. Thomas quit school after the fourth grade, and headed for the city's old vaudeville and movie house neighborhoods. He was a smart youth, so he quickly got a part-time job selling snacks in one of the movie houses. He got to meet many well-known entertainers, including blues singers Ma Rainey and Bessie Smith. Within a short time, he learned to pick out tunes he heard at the movie houses on his mother's organ.

But the most important gift for him was the privilege of knowing the theater's pianists and learning from them. According to Dr. Michael Harris in his book *The Rise of Gospel Blues,* young Thomas also learned how "to support the harmony of a song,"[5] develop camaraderie and discipline, and help "develop an identity that would bring him respect."[6] By the time Thomas was a teenager, he was playing for rowdy house parties, dances, and low-end nightclubs.

✦ **Harmony** comes from the pleasing sound of a combination of musical notes played simultaneously.

When poor African Americans left the South and headed north in the Black Migration during and after World War I to seek a better life, Dorsey went, too. He ended up in the Chicago–Gary, Indiana, area in 1919, where he put together a small band. Chicago after World War I was a magnet for musicians who wanted to be successful and famous.

The young jazz trumpeter Louis Armstrong, jazz pianist Jelly Roll Morton, ragtime piano innovator Scott Joplin, bluesman W. C. Handy, and a host of other musicians went to Chicago to be a part of the growing musical scene and pursue success.

As early as 1921, Dorsey began creating his own special mixture of "bouncy melodies with a religious theme,"[7] and called them gospel songs. He also began attending annual meetings of the National Baptist Convention in Chicago.

Dorsey continued to play in shady, rowdy dance halls, and at boisterous rent parties. Rent parties are gatherings where the attendees raise money to help the renter pay his or her rent. Dorsey also wrote music for and traveled with blues stars Ma Rainey and Stovepipe Johnson. He co-led the Whispering Syncopators big band, and co-created popular, catchy tunes under the nickname Georgia Tom.

When the 1929 stock market crash brought joblessness and poverty to the country, Dorsey turned more toward religious music and to the church, the community's most stable institution, offering hope and comfort to its beleaguered citizens. He settled in at Ebenezer Baptist Church where he organized the world's first gospel choir. He also co-founded the Chicago Gospel Choral Union.

In 1932, he was appointed chorus director at Pilgrim Baptist Church, and he also opened his own Dorsey House of Music. He founded the National Convention of Gospel Choirs and Choruses with gospel singer Sallie Martin, and within a few years had an annual attendance of 10,000 to 15,000 delegates.

Dorsey remembered the impression that "moanin" had made on him as a child and incorporated it into his unique blend of religious and bluesy arrangements and compositions. Moanin', an emotional, religious staple in black and especially Baptist congregations, comes from something spiritual inside a worshiper until the singer(s) and the congregation have to holler and shout Hallelujah. And though Dorsey couldn't define it, he knew how to compose it.

Dorsey made extensive use of moanin' in his music, especially with the song "Amazing Grace," written by John Newton, a white former slave-ship owner who experienced a religious conversion and then wrote the now famous song.

In 1932, Dorsey suffered a tragedy that acutely tested his faith—the deaths of both his wife, Nettie Harper, and his newborn son, Thomas Jr., in one week. His "fight for faith" in the wake of that double tragedy led him to write "Precious Lord, Take My Hand," the song nearer than any other to him. According to gospel historian Gwendolin Sims Warren, Dorsey says the words of his most famous song "came twisting out of my very heart,"[8] and he almost gave up writing gospel music.

This song has since been translated into more than fifty languages, has been sung by every major African American gospel singer, and has become a hit for white country-and-western singers.

Before he died on January 23, 1993, in Chicago, Dorsey had written over 800 gospel songs, as well as many blues songs—though he had stopped creating and performing jazz and blues tunes long ago.

JAMES CLEVELAND—THE KING OF GOSPEL

James Cleveland, another great gospel singer and musical innovator, was a Chicago native. The man who had been christened the King of Gospel music by his peers and admirers began singing in church at age eight. As a young boy, he delivered newspapers to the home of gospel singer Mahalia Jackson, whom he greatly admired. James first heard Thomas A. Dorsey, the Father of Gospel Music, when his grandmother started taking him to Dorsey's church. After listening to Dorsey's beautiful gospels, James was inspired and recalls that he made black and white keys from the "wedges and crevices" he found on the windowsill at home and began teaching himself to play the piano. Cleveland, who was well known for his gravelly voice and bluesy-gospel sound, earned a star on the Hollywood Walk of Fame for "Peace Be Still," one of his most successful songs.

Part Four

Modern Times

LOUIS "SATCHMO" ARMSTRONG

(1901–1971)

✦

Trumpeter Louis "Satchmo" Armstrong was probably the most influential jazz musician of his time. With his gravelly voice, gleaming smile, and golden horn, the man whom many have called the Ambassador of Jazz showcased American music to the world for over fifty years.

New Orleans was an international seaport and a fertile ground for the many types of orchestras, brass bands, marching bands, blues, and jazz music that were being created at the time. Louis Armstrong was born there on August 4, 1901,[1] to Maryann Armstrong, a domestic worker, and Willie Armstrong, a turpentine factory worker. They lived in a crowded part of New Orleans called James Alley in the Back o' Town section with Willie Armstrong's mother, Mrs. Josephine Armstrong. When young Louis's parents separated, his grandmother raised him. She taught him right from wrong and took him to church, where he learned to sing. When describing himself as a child, Armstrong would often say, "I stayed in my place, I respected everybody and I was never rude or sassy."[2]

From time to time during his early childhood, Louis also lived with his mother, new baby sister, and several stepfathers. The family was very poor, and Louis sold newspapers, sang in quartets on street corners for change from pimps, prostitutes, and musicians, and occasionally even gambled for pennies with his friends.

On New Year's Eve when Louis was twelve or thirteen, he took his stepfather Slim's gun out of the house and shot it several times in the air to celebrate the New Year. He was arrested, spent a miserable night in jail, and ended up at the Colored Waifs Home for Boys, where Louis learned discipline, stability, and how to play the bugle and the cornet. He left a year later, "proud of the days I spent at the Colored Waifs Home for Boys."[3]

When Louis was seventeen, he formed his own six-man orchestra. When they played, they swore they sounded as good as jazzmen Joe "King" Oliver and Edward "Kid" Ory, the two hottest bandleaders in New Orleans at the time. Oliver became Louis's mentor (Armstrong called Oliver his "fairy godfather") and even gave the teenager one of his own cornets. In 1922, Armstrong moved to Chicago, where Oliver had relocated, and played second cornet in Oliver's band. He then moved to New York, where he played in Fletcher Henderson's band. Henderson suggested that he switch to the trumpet, and he did. Louis stayed with that instrument the rest of his life.

By the mid-1920s, jazz's popularity soared as a result of the development of records and radio. Armstrong's *Heebie Jeebies* album, released in 1926 by Okeh Records, introduced his unique scat singing style to the public. Although Armstrong wrote original music, he was mostly featured with big bands. He also wrote "I Wish I Could Shimmy Like My Sister Kate" but wasn't credited or paid for it.

✦ When you use your voice like an instrument, singing nonsense syllables for jazzy notes, you are **scat singing.**

A colorful speaker and a prolific writer with an engaging sense of humor, Louis often called his associates Pops and signed his letters "Red beans and ricely yours," a reference to his favorite meal.

Louis Armstrong was known throughout the world. He appeared in some sixty movies, including *Pennies from Heaven* (1936) and *Hello Dolly* (1969). He toured Europe and Africa, and recorded thousands of songs individually and with other singers Ella Fitzgerald and Billie Holiday. A role model for aspiring musicians, he won over 200 awards, received honorary doctorates, and traveled as a cultural ambassador of goodwill for the U.S. State Department.

Armstrong died in his sleep at his home in Queens, New York, on July 6, 1971, after suffering a heart attack earlier that year. His home, now a city and national landmark, is the Louis Armstrong House and Archives run by Queens College, City University of New York. African nations have honored Louis Armstrong with postage stamps, and the United States issued a Louis Armstrong postage stamp in 1995.

Born into extreme poverty at the turn of the century, Louis Armstrong's life is proof that with determination, hope, hard work, common sense, and sacrifice, any young boy or girl can one day become a black star.

Armstrong's music lives on today. Moviegoers can hear him sing "What a Wonderful World" in the movie *Good Morning, Vietnam,* and "Talk to the Animals" in Eddie Murphy's film version of *Dr. Dolittle.*

The Pioneer

When Louis Armstrong was interviewed by Larry King in 1967 for a magazine article, Armstrong recalls that "as time went on and I made a reputation, I had it put in my contracts that I wouldn't play no place I couldn't stay. I was the first Negro in the business to crack them big white hotels—Oh yeah! I pioneered, Pops! Nobody much remembers that these days."[4]

MAHALIA JACKSON

(1912–1972)

Mahalia Jackson, popularly known as the Queen of Gospel, said she always sang her religious songs the way she heard them played in New Orleans by brass bands leading funerals to graveyards and back. Coming back, "they would all get right into the jubilant feeling of this jazzy music. So that's how a lot of our songs that I sing today has that type of beat, because it's my inheritance, things that I've always been doing, born and raised-up and seen, that went on in New Orleans."[1]

One of six children, Mahalia Jackson was born in a poor section of New Orleans near the Mississippi River on October 26, 1912. Her parents were Charity Clark Jackson, a laundress, and Johnny Jackson, a Baptist preacher, dockworker, and barber. Mahalia was a singer from the time she was five years old. Her home church, Mount Moriah Baptist, was a "foot-tapping and hand-clapping" church that "gave her the bounce."[2]

The sanctified church next door gave her "a powerful beat, a rhythm we held onto from slavery days,"[3] which she would

incorporate into her music for the rest of her career. Her mother died when she was five. Her father sent her and her older brother to live with her aunt, Mahalia Paul (nicknamed Aunt Duke), after whom she was named. Aunt Duke was a strict disciplinarian.

As a child, Mahalia never had a store-bought doll. She made rag dolls with braided grass for hair. She scrubbed floors with lye, made mattresses, gathered firewood with a wheelbarrow and an ax, and picked up lumps of coal from the railroad tracks for winter fuel. She also worked in white folks' houses helping their children get dressed, and washing dishes for $2 a week. Because Mahalia had to quit school at an early age to work, she always considered herself "one of the last of the Old School of Negroes"[4] who "had to make it without education."[5]

Growing up, Mahalia was influenced by the popular brass bands, showboats cruising on the Mississippi River, and "corner" bands playing ragtime, jazz, and blues music on every corner. Mahalia was not allowed to attend dances or hang out in the streets. But while Aunt Duke was at work, Mahalia and her cousin Fred, Aunt Duke's grown son, would listen to Ma Rainey and Bessie Smith records on a windup phonograph. Two of Mahalia's favorites were the W. C. Handy song "St. Louis Blues" and "Careless Love," both sung by Bessie Smith.

She recalls, "I'd fix my mouth and try to make my tones come out just like hers. . . . And I'd whisper to myself that someday the sun was going to shine down on me way up North in Chicago or Kansas City or one of those other faraway places."[6]

By age sixteen, Mahalia had moved to Chicago, which would remain her home for the rest of her life. The Chicago Mahalia saw when she arrived looked like another world: black men wearing stylish spats and derbies, carrying walking sticks; the women wearing fur coats and walking dogs on leashes. Many owned mansions on Michigan Avenue, had diamonds and silks, and drove Rolls-Royces. But the black church "was the core" of Negro social life.

Mahalia dreamed of becoming a nurse while singing for the Lord, but shortly after she arrived in Chicago, the stock market crashed and good-paying jobs for everybody became scarce. Southern black people like Mahalia, who had migrated to Chicago during the 1920s to find better jobs, suffered.

Mahalia kept singing and holding on to every penny she could find—and there weren't many. Doing domestic work brought in only $12 a week. But she stuck it out, joined Greater Salem Baptist church, and began singing in the choirs. Singing gospel lifted her heart and kept her from becoming depressed and angry over how hard it was to survive.

Mahalia joined the Johnson Gospel Singers through her church. Sometimes they got $1.50 each per night for their performances. Soon they were singing all over Chicago, and beyond, and Mahalia became popular as a soloist. By the middle of the Depression, she was traveling outside of Chicago, from New York to California.

By the early 1930s, gospel music was beginning to capture the attention of black congregations. It took hold of Mahalia Jackson, too. In Chicago, she met Thomas A. Dorsey, onetime blues composer, now a popular church choirmaster. The songs he composed were known as "gospel blues," and would earn him the title of Father of the Gospel Blues. After meeting Dorsey, she traveled around the country with him during the late 1930s and early 1940s, singing his gospel songs, which included his most popular composition, "Precious Lord, Take My Hand." Her first recording came in 1934 with her successful "God's Gonna Separate the Wheat from the Tares," followed by the Reverend W. Herbert Brewster composition "Move On Up a Little Higher," which she recorded in 1947 for Apollo Records. It sold over 2 million copies shortly after its release.

Mahalia drew audiences with performances "in her deeply individualistic manner—running and skipping down the church and concert hall aisles, her eyes closed, hands tightly clasped, with feet tapping and body throbbing, all the while her voice soaring as if there were no walls to confine its spiritual journey—she was utterly possessed and possessing. It was pure theater."[7]

Ed Sullivan invited her to appear on his show in 1950. Her record "I Can Put My Trust in Jesus" won an award from the French Academy of Music in 1952. In 1954, she got her own radio show on a CBS radio affiliate in Chicago. A year later, it became a television show.

Despite her successes in Europe and the United States, Mahalia still had to deal with the racism she constantly encountered in this country.

When she bought a house in a middle-class, predominantly white neighborhood in Chicago, angry whites shot through the windows shortly after she moved in. And like Louis Armstrong, she could not perform in many places, including places in her own hometown of New Orleans, until after the mid-1960s.

By 1947, she had become the first "Official" Gospel Singer for the National Baptist Convention. Among the many black Baptist leaders she met through the conventions was the Reverend Martin Luther King Jr., whom she came to regard as a close friend. As their friendship and the civil rights movement of the 1950s and 1960s grew, Jackson began to see her "voice as a weapon for change."[8]

She sang for King and other SCLC and NAACP officials at rallies and functions, including the historic August 28, 1963, March on Washington. Her selection was "I Been 'Buked and I Been Scorned," a Mahalia Jackson trademark, and one of Dr. King's favorites.

When she first sang in Carnegie Hall in New York, she shared the stage with gospel singers Rosetta Tharp, the Gaye Sisters, Clara Ward, Roberta Martin, and others. The audience broke all house records.

By 1955, she had moved from Apollo Records to Columbia, and had hosted her first thirty-minute radio show for Columbia. When she performed "He's Got the Whole World in His Hands" on the Dinah Shore television show, offers started pouring in. In 1958, she sang again in the re-release of the movie *Imitation of Life.*

Despite her popularity, whites in the television and recording industry kept strict control over and placed many commercial restrictions on Mahalia Jackson's singing. She often complained, not only about those restrictions but also about the commercialization of black gospel.

Mahalia Jackson married Isaac Hockenhull in 1938. Although they soon divorced, they remained friends throughout the rest of their lives. In 1964 or 1965, she married Sigmund "Minters" Galloway, a widower. They divorced in 1967. Mahalia never had children. She did help raise a child who became known as Brother John Sellers, a gospel and blues singer.

Jackson was also a successful entrepreneur. She studied hairdressing at the Madame C. J. Walker's and Scott Institute of Beauty Culture and owned and operated Mahalia's Beauty Salon as well as Mahalia's House of Flowers (a florist shop) while pursuing a musical career. She later started the Mahalia Jackson Food System, a business that produced some twenty-five varieties of food through A&P's canning plants.

By 1963, Mahalia Jackson's health began to fail. She died in Little Company of Mary Hospital in Evergreen Park outside Chicago on January 27, 1972, and was buried in New Orleans. Among her many awards and recognitions is her induction into the Rock and Roll Hall of Fame in Cleveland, Ohio. She recorded more than thirty albums, sang at President John F. Kennedy's 1961 inauguration gala ceremonies and at the historic 1963 March on Washington for Jobs and Freedom, and won a number of Grammies and other awards.

Mahalia Jackson stayed "with the songs that came out of the swamps and cane fields and from around the railroad tracks . . . "[9] throughout her career. She once said, "A song must do something for me as well as for the people that hear it. I can't sing a song that doesn't have a message. If it doesn't have the strength it can't lift you."[10]

SHIRLEY CAESAR—
THE NEW FIRST LADY OF GOSPEL

Shirley Caesar was born on October 13, 1938, in Durham, North Carolina. A gospel singer since childhood, Caesar is called the "premiere gospel diva of our time."[11] She is also known as the First Lady of Gospel and the Queen of Gospel, titles first given to Mahalia Jackson. She is an internationally known singer, songwriter, evangelist, and minister, a Broadway religious musical star, and the winner of numerous Grammies and other national awards. Caesar is a traditional gospel singer, and her concerts around the world combine sermons with songs as well as call and response with her audiences. Caesar, who still lives in North Carolina, sings the kind of gospel music "that was born out of hard times, born out of slavery, born out of being beat into doing things you did not want to do."[12]

✦ **Call and response** is when a leader sings out the main line or phrase, and the congregation or group answers with either the same or another set of words "in response."

ELLA FITZGERALD

(1917-1996)

Singer Ella Jane Fitzgerald was born on April 25, 1917, in the southern coastal town of Newport News, Virginia. Her parents were William and Tempie Williams Fitzgerald. While she was still a small child, Ella, her mother, stepfather, and half-sister, Frances, moved to Yonkers, New York.

Young Ella's first love was dancing. She liked to dance so much, she was nicknamed Snakehips after Earl "Snakehips" Tucker, a popular Cotton Club dancer. Music was always in Ella's home, and she was especially attracted to the music of the Mills Brothers, Louis Armstrong, and the New Orleans Boswell Sisters. She absorbed what she admired most, and then used it to develop her own style.

When Ella was fifteen, her mother died, and the grieving teenager went to live with an aunt in Harlem. Unhappy and unable to live with her aunt, she ran away.

Believing in herself and determined to succeed, Ella entered a talent show at the then newly opened—and now famous—Apollo Theater on November 1, 1934, in New York. Because some of the dance competitors

were dressed in much fancier clothing than hers, she decided to sing instead, and won first place. Her second break came in 1935 when she auditioned for drummer and bandleader Chick Webb and became a singer in his band. That year, she recorded "Love and Kisses" and "I'll Chase the Blues Away" with the band.

In 1937, Ella was voted the Number One Female Vocalist in the first Down Beat and Melody Maker readers' polls. Her first big hit was "A-Tisket, A-Tasket," a nonsense song that she wrote. By the summer of 1938, it went to number one on the famous Hit Parade list and stayed there for nineteen months. By 1950, it had sold over a million copies.

In 1939, after her friend Chick Webb died, Ella took over the band and renamed it Ella Fitzgerald and Her Famous Orchestra. She kept the band going until 1942. She made her first movie with the comedy team of Abbott and Costello in the 1942 film *Ride 'Em Cowboy.*

In 1946, she made her first recording with her idol, Louis Armstrong. They recorded "You Won't Be Satisfied" and "The Frim Fram Sauce" with Decca Records. They also recorded "Lady Be Good" in March 1947, when she gave her signature scat performance for the first time. As usual, Ms. Fitzgerald had listened to Armstrong, Leo Watson, and other singers scat singing, and developed her own unique and recognizable scatting style.

✦ **Bebop** is a form of music that has very "complicated chords," and "long strings of notes" are played so fast that the rhythms "are almost impossible to dance to."[1]

As World War II ended, big bands began to fade away. But by then she was captivated with a new movement called bebop. The new sound became a part of her repertoire, and she formed her own bebop trio. In December of 1947, she married musician Ray Brown. They divorced in 1953.

In February 1949, Ms. Fitzgerald joined some of the country's top jazz musicians on Norman Krantz's popular Jazz at the Philharmonic concert series tours. Her song "How High the Moon" became a Jazz at the Philharmonic signature tune. Krantz became her manager in

December 1953, and by the next year, she had sold over 22 million records for Decca. In 1955, she signed with Verve Records and stayed with them until 1966.

Fitzgerald recorded more albums with Louis Armstrong, including *Ella and Louis* in 1957 and *Porgy and Bess* in 1958 for Verve Records. She also appeared in the 1958 star-studded movie *St. Louis Blues*. She is well known for the 1950s recordings of her "Songbooks," albums that featured the music of such mainstream luminaries as George and Ira Gershwin, Irving Berlin, Cole Porter, and Duke Ellington. She won her first Grammy award in 1958 for Best Vocal Performance by a Female

THREE JAZZ DIVAS

Billie Holiday, Sarah Vaughan, and Ella Fitzgerald were contemporaries, and their singing styles were often compared.

Billie Holiday was born Eleanora Fagan on April 7, 1915, in Baltimore, Maryland, to Clarence Holiday and Sadie Fagan. Her father called her Bill because he thought of her as a tomboy. She turned it into Billie after a movie star, and took on her father's last name.[2] She became a legendary jazz and blues singer who has influenced many singers. Holiday sang mood songs that reflected the heartache and problems in her life.

Billie Holiday died on July 17, 1959, from illnesses brought on by her addiction to heroin.

Sarah Lois Vaughan was born on March 27, 1924, in Newark, New Jersey. Like many entertainers, including Ella Fitzerald, she began her career when she won an Apollo Theater amateur contest in 1942. Like Ella Fitzgerald, she became a premiere jazz and pop singer. She was nicknamed the Divine Sarah, the Divine One, and Sassy Sarah. Although Sarah Vaughan was probably best known for her songs "Broken-Hearted Melody," "Misty," and "Just One of Those Things," she was also an accomplished pianist. She died on April 3, 1990, at her home in California. In 1999, the city of Newark renamed the street where the New Jersey Performing Arts Center sits Sarah Vaughan Way.

and Best Jazz Performance for the *Duke Ellington Songbook.* In 1974, the University of Maryland named a new campus facility for her: the Ella Fitzgerald Center for the Performing Arts.

Though the rock-and-roll era of the 1960s and early 1970s pushed her to the background, Fitzgerald continued recording and traveling around the world. This hectic schedule eventually took its toll on her health. By 1972, she had developed diabetes and had surgery on her right eye to remove a cataract. Not yet ready to retire, she went to London to perform, and in February 1976 she won her eighth Grammy for *Fitzgerald and Pass [Joe]. . . Again.* When at age sixty-four she became an audiotape company's "Memorex Lady" ("Is it Ella or is it Memorex?"), fans who loved her songs in the 1930s, 1940s, and 1950s remained loyal, and new fans were enjoying her for the first time.

Fitzgerald's health problems continued. She had open-heart surgery in 1986 and a toe amputated in 1987 due to her diabetes, but she continued performing. In 1988, she traveled to Rome and recorded the album *Ella in Rome: The Birthday Concert.* It went to number one on the *Billboard* chart, and she called it her best work since *Porgy.*

By the 1990s, the First Lady of Song had received so many awards, including a National Medal of Arts from President Reagan in 1987, that they filled up a whole room in her Beverly Hills, California, home.

Ella Fitzgerald died on June 16, 1996, in Beverly Hills.

The Divine Sarah Vaughan as a young performer at the mike, singing the music she loved for the world to enjoy and keep on enjoying for years to come.

B. B. KING

(B. 1925)

In the 1940s, a sound known as rhythm and blues (R&B) grew out of the mixing of country blues, gospel, black big band sound, black doo-wop singing groups, St. Louis–style honky-tonk, and the ageless beat of the African drum. R&B is acknowledged as the source of today's pop, soul, rock-and-roll, rock, and rap music.

Riley "B. B." King and his beloved Gibson guitar, Lucille, have influenced and inspired R&B musicians all over the world.

B. B. King was born on a plantation near Itta Bena and Indianola, Mississippi, on September 16, 1925, to Albert King and Nora Ella Pully King. His parents separated while he was a child. He lived with his mother, who loved to sing, and his grandmother in Kilmichael, Mississippi, where he sang in church choirs and school quartets.

Little Riley loved listening to records on his Aunt Mim's windup phonograph player. He listened to Texas blues guitarist "Blind Lemon" Jefferson and blues singers Bessie Smith and Ma Rainey. The first guitar Riley ever touched belonged to a minister who told him the guitar was a "precious instrument," and "another way to express God's

love."[1] Young Riley would make "guitars" by tying strands of wire onto broomsticks, and then make believe he was playing a real one.

When he was nine years old, his mother died. For a time, the grieving child lived with his grandmother, but she soon died, too. So little Riley, at about age ten, moved into an empty cabin on the nearby Cartledge plantation, where he worked as a farmhand making $15 a month.

When he was twelve, he bought his first guitar for $15 and taught himself to play by following an instruction book he bought from a Sears Roebuck catalogue. King recalls in his autobiography, *Blues All Around Me,* "that guitar gave me new life. It helped me cope."[2] One day, someone stole his guitar from his cabin.

Riley also lived with his father, stepmother, three stepsisters, and stepbrother in Lexington, Kentucky, for about six months. He was so unhappy, however, that in 1938 he ran away to live with relatives near Indianola.

Throughout his childhood, Riley had heard the blues and field songs but had been forbidden to sing them. During the Depression and pre–World War II years, churchgoing folks considered the blues to be the devil's music. And although Riley enjoyed listening to Duke Ellington, Count Basie, Louis Armstrong, and other musical greats on the radio, he was planning to be a preacher or a gospel singer. He joined the famous St. John Gospel Singers, but whenever he could, he would sing and play the blues in the juke joints and clubs of Indianola.

In 1944, during World War II, Riley married Martha Lee and enlisted in the U.S. Army. His time in the military was an unhappy experience because of the racism he encountered from the white officers. After the war ended, King returned to Indianola, but after accidentally damaging his boss's tractor, soon moved on to Memphis, Tennessee, and its famous Beale Street. In Memphis, he dived into playing and singing the blues. When he wasn't playing in Bobby "Blue" Bland's band or in bars and clubs in the area, Riley worked for WDIA as a DJ on his own radio show, which was sponsored by Pepticon. Pepticon was a tonic that, like the blues, was supposed to cure folks of anything that made them feel bad.

✦**DJ** is the abbreviation for disc jockey, or deejay. Fast-talking, entertaining, record-playing radio announcers began calling themselves **DJ**s in the 1940s and 1950s.

King became known as the Pepticon Boy. By 1953, the nickname changed to Blues Boy from Beale Street. It changed again to Beale Street Blues Boy, then to Blues Boy, and finally to simply B. B. During his radio days, he played the songs of the great blues, jazz, and R&B singers such as Dinah Washington, Little Esther Phillips, and Nat "King" Cole.

After playing in the clubs and on the radio, King was eager to begin recording songs. He recorded four songs in 1949 and named one after his wife, Martha Lee. In 1951–1952, he had his first hit record when "Three O'Clock Blues" climbed to the top of the rhythm-and-blues charts. B. B. King and his band became increasingly popular with black audiences and the chitlin circuit with rhythm-and-blues hits like "Every Day I Have the Blues" in the 1950s and "Rock Me, Baby" in 1964.

When younger black audiences began turning away from the blues, King and other blues and R&B players like Muddy Waters and John Lee Hooker realized that the young white British and American population were discovering and loving blues music. He and his band began headlining rock festivals with English guitarist Eric Clapton, American rock group Jefferson Airplane, white blues singer Janis Joplin, and dozens of other acts. His biggest hit came in 1969 with "The Thrill Is Gone," which combined blues and orchestra strings, and earned him a Grammy Award. The song is now a recognized classic.

B. B. King is the father of fifteen children. He supports community and civil rights causes and performs regularly at prisons. He won the 1984 Grammy for best traditional blues recording, and a 1988 Lifetime Achievement Award. He has been inducted into the Songwriters Hall of Fame; received a Presidential Medal of Freedom from George Bush, and a National Heritage Fellowship Award from the National Endowment for the Arts. King has performed all over the world. Despite having diabetes, he continues to tour extensively.

B. B. King, the Ambassador of the Blues, was inducted into the Ebony Magazine Blues Hall of Fame in 1974, the Blues Foundation Hall of Fame in 1980, the Rock and Roll Hall of Fame in 1987, and has a star on Hollywood's Walk of Fame. He also owns a popular night-club on Beale Street called B. B. King's Blues Club and Restaurant.

Muddy Waters—The Delta Bluesman

One of the best-known professional bluesmen was McKinley Morganfield, also known as Muddy Waters. He was born in Rolling Fork, Mississippi, on April 4, 1915, to Ollie and Bertha Jones Morganfield. From around age three, he lived with his grand-mother on the Stovall plantation outside Clarksdale, Mississippi, where the presence of blues music was strong. His grandmother nicknamed him Muddy because he played in the mud all the time; kids added on Waters, and the name stuck.

As a child, Muddy Waters worked hard in the fields, making pennies a day and listening to work songs, field hollers, and blues music from harmonicas and guitars. He began playing harmonica as a boy, and later, the guitar. Folklorist Alan Lomax was so impressed with his music that he recorded Waters in 1941 and 1942 for the Library of Congress Archives of American Folk Songs.

Around 1943, when Muddy Waters's boss refused to give him a raise, Waters headed for Chicago, where his voice and electric blues guitar playing became a Chicago blues trademark. His song "Rolling Stone" became such a worldwide folk and rock classic that a popular music magazine and a British rock band named themselves after it. Known worldwide as a true bluesman from the Delta, Waters produced dozens of albums, including *I'm Your Hoochie Coochie Man* and *Got My Mojo Workin'.*

Muddy Waters died of a heart attack in his sleep at his Westmont, Illinois, home just outside Chicago on April 30, 1983.

CHUCK BERRY

(B. 1926)

The true King of Rock and Roll, Chuck Berry is a tall, slender, well-coiffed composer and singer-guitarist who took the sounds of Missouri-style honky-tonk, blues, and Baptist choir music, and his own experience of being a teenager in St. Louis and turned them into songs that white teenagers around the world in the 1950s loved.

Charles Edward Anderson Berry was the fourth of six children born to Henry and Martha Banks Berry on October 18, 1926, in the bedroom of his parents' three-room brick cottage in the Elleardsville section of black St. Louis. As a child, Chuck was fascinated by the family piano, which his mother played, and the Victrola (a trademark name for a phonograph). Once he climbed up on a chair and turned on the Victrola. When he heard his mother coming, he turned it back off but forgot to move the chair. Mrs. Berry gave Chuck a "whoopin'" (whipping) and a warning, "Be sure your sins will find you out," a "verbal chastisement" that he would hear again and again, "whenever I was caught, in mischief."[1]

Though times were hard in Depression-era St. Louis, the Berry

family maintained a fairly comfortable lifestyle. Henry Berry, a carpenter, also worked in a flour mill. Martha Berry, a college graduate who once aspired to be a schoolteacher, stayed home to take care of their growing family. The Berry family were devoted churchgoers of Antioch Baptist Church.

The Antioch choir would meet for practice regularly in the Berry home, and the choir always enjoyed watching little Chuck duckwalk. He would stoop with fully bended knees and, with straight back and upright head, duckwalk under the table and reach for his toys. Years later, this duckwalk became famous when the adult Chuck Berry performed it onstage while playing his guitar.

Berry attended nearby Cottage Avenue Elementary School. By age twelve, he was 5 feet, 11 inches tall. He loved listening to country music, boogie-woogie, blues, and gospel choirs such as Wings Over Jordan on the radio. He and his brother, Henry, and sister, Lucy, sang in a gospel group called the Jubilee Ensembles. By the time he entered all-black Sumner High School, he had developed an interest in photography.

✦ **Boogie-woogie** music is a fast form of blues played on piano and sometimes accompanied by an orchestra.

When he was about fourteen, he performed in an All Men's Review. Accompanied by a band member on a guitar, he sang Kansas City bandleader Jay McShann's popular tune "Confessin' the Blues." This was the beginning of his desire to become a performer. He was determined that one day he would be singing and accompanying himself on the guitar. A classmate lent him his first guitar, a four-string tenor.

While still a teenager, Chuck worked with his dad doing carpentry. He also began deejaying for black soldiers at the local USO center, and was playing and singing at backyard parties. He owned his own car, and was popular with the girls.

He married Themetta Suggs in 1948. Berry began training seriously on the guitar, and guitarist Ira Harris helped him develop his very own style. He also studied books on guitar playing to improve his playing. By June of 1952, Chuck Berry was playing with his friend Tommy Stevens's combo at Huff's Garden in St. Louis. He was soon asked to join his friend Johnnie Johnson's Sir John's Trio to play a New Year's Eve party at the Cosmopolitan Club across the Mississippi River in East St. Louis, Illinois. It wasn't long before people started noticing Berry's playing.

He continued working with his father in the carpentry business. But determined to make a career in music, Berry traveled to Chicago, Illinois, in 1955. He soon met blues singer Muddy Waters, whom he called the Godfather of the Blues, and who was his "greatest inspiration" in helping him launch his career. Waters sent Berry to Leonard Chess of Chess Records. The song Berry played for Chess was called "Ida May." The Chess label released the song as "Maybellene," and after it played on Alan Freed's New York radio program, it became Berry's first big hit in 1955. At the time, Berry was not given credit for writing the song, and he did not receive much in royalty payments. It took Berry about thirty years to recover his full rights to the song.

He followed his hit "Maybellene" with another best-seller called "Roll Over Beethoven," which hit the national charts in 1956. The Beatles would later record this song. When Berry went on tour that year, he performed the duckwalk onstage, and it became his trademark.

Berry composed many more best-selling songs. He wrote "Too Much Monkey Business" (1956), "School Days" and "Rock 'n Roll Music" (1957), "Sweet Little Sixteen" (1958), and "Johnny B. Goode" (1958). "Johnny B. Goode" was placed aboard the *Voyager* space probes sent into outer space in 1977.

Berry, who also learned to be a wise businessman and investor, earned enough money from his record sales and national tours to buy several acres of farmland outside the St. Louis suburb of Wentzville. He built a large home for his entire family, complete with outdoor stadium, studio, and amusement park, and called it Berry Park.

Berry also went to court over the Beach Boys' 1963 hit "Surfin' U.S.A.," which "so blatantly appropriated the melody and rhythm of Berry's 'Sweet Little Sixteen' that he sued and won a songwriting credit."[2]

In 1968, he bought a building in Wentzville with the intent of opening a theater, but local racism caused the theater to close. He later bought a Wentzville restaurant called the Southern Aire, but was forced to close it. Despite these and other problems, Chuck Berry continued making music. He went on to record his biggest hit of all in 1972—"My Ding-a-Ling."

Many major rock-and-roll stars and aspiring bands have recorded one of Berry's songs. Called the "folk poet" of the 1950s, this black star was inducted into the Blues Foundation Hall of Fame in 1985. On January 23, 1986, he was inducted into the Rock and Roll Hall of Fame. In 1989, he was inducted into the St. Louis Walk of Fame, with a star embedded in the sidewalk at 6504 Delmar in front of the Blueberry Hill Bar and Restaurant. Each year, Chuck Berry visits Blueberry Hill and performs his legendary music.

LITTLE RICHARD

Richard Wayne Penniman was born on December 25, 1935, in Macon, Georgia. This flamboyant rock-and-roll innovator was the creator of the popular 1950s songs "Good Golly, Miss Molly," "Long, Tall Sally," and "Tutti-Frutti, Aw-Rootie." This minister and pop singer's famous high-pitched "woooo" and "shut up!", heavy facial makeup, and bold clothing have made him a classic of the rock-and-roll era.

RAY CHARLES

(B. 1930)

In the late 1950s and early 1960s, the civil rights movement led to an increased awareness in and celebration of the everyday musical life of African Americans as well. Black church shouts, blues, and rhythm-and-blues music became more acceptable, for a time.

In this active and changing time in American society, a young blind musician named Ray Charles Robinson set the radio airwaves on fire, and introduced the new name of "soul music" to an old musical sound.

The legendary Ray Charles was born sighted to Bailey Robinson, a handyman, and Aretha Robinson, a laundress, on September 23, 1930, in Albany, Georgia. Ray and his family moved to Greenville, Florida, when he was still a child. His love of music came from the blues, church gospel, jazz, boogie-woogie, and country-and-western music he heard around him in his neighborhood. Ray recalls that at age three he was taught to play simple melodies on the piano by a "wonderful man" named Wylie Pitman.

When he was about four or five years old, he saw his younger

brother, Georgie, drown after falling into a tub of washwater in the family's yard. Shortly after that trauma, Ray began losing his vision, probably due to the disease glaucoma. When doctors told Ray's mother he would lose all his sight, she began helping her son learn to deal with his impending blindness by showing him how to get around and find things. By the time he was seven, his sight was gone.

Though Mrs. Robinson only had a fifth-grade education, she was determined that Ray would grow up to be self-sufficient and independent. "He's blind, but he ain't stupid," Mrs. Robinson said. "He's lost his sight but he ain't lost his mind."[1] She sent him to the racially segregated St. Augustine School for the Deaf and Blind in Florida. At age twelve, he wrote his first musical arrangement. The first instruments he learned to play included the clarinet and the piano. He would read three or four bars of music in Braille, then play it, practice it, and memorize it.

Ray's mother died when he was fifteen, and the grieving teen left St. Augustine's. For the next few years, he stayed with family friends in Florida while he played in various bands, including a hillbilly band called The Florida Playboys. While playing with them, he learned to yodel. Ray eventually ended up in Seattle, Washington, where he formed his first trio and dropped his last name to avoid confusion with fighter "Sugar" Ray Robinson.

In 1959, Charles's song "What I Say" became a crossover pop hit, and white audiences were now grooving to Ray Charles's soulful tunes. He followed that hit with another crossover hit called "Drown in My Own Tears." During the 1970s, Charles, who was a shrewd businessman, started up his own recording labels. He called one of them Crossover.

✦ Music that begins in one category for one audience but becomes so popular that it appeals to a lot more people is a **crossover** hit.

Charles has repeatedly felt the sting of racism throughout his career. During the 1950s, at a scheduled concert in Augusta, Georgia, he discovered that the audience was to be segregated—the black audience upstairs, the whites downstairs. Charles objected. "I told the promoter that I didn't mind segregation, except that he had it backwards. After all, I was black and it only made sense to have the black folk close to me."[2] Ray Charles refused to play. The promoter sued Charles and won.

But Ray Charles held firm to his principles. He was a devoted supporter of civil rights, and a good friend and financial backer of the Reverend Doctor Martin Luther King Jr.

He also made his feelings about racism and segregation known through his music. He recorded albums such as *A Message from the People* in the 1970s, and other protest songs, including "Danger Zone" and "You're In for a Big Surprise." He was quoted in the *Encyclopedia of Pop, Rock and Soul* as saying, "I was recording protest songs when it wasn't a popular thing to do."[3]

Ray Charles, the outspoken musician, being interviewed by Eleanora E. Tate, the author of this book.

In addition to rhythm and blues and jazz, Ray Charles also recorded and popularized a number of country-and-western songs. His haunting rendition of "Georgia on My Mind" in 1960 became the official Georgia state song. His sultry female backup group, the Raelets, set the standard for black vocal groups such as the Shirelles, the Supremes, and Martha and the Vandellas. He has a star on Hollywood Boulevard's Walk of Fame. He was honored with a bronze medallion by the French Republic. He has won over twelve Grammies and was inducted into the Rock and Roll Hall of Fame in 1986.

Ray Charles is one of the major visionaries of 1960s soul music, and has influenced every soul singer who came after him. British singers Mick Jagger, Joe Cocker, and Rod Stewart point to Ray Charles as their inspiration. Singer Nina Simone, bebop trumpeter Dizzy Gillespie, jazz saxophonists Charlie Parker and John Coltrane, and contemporary composer Quincy Jones have all embraced and been inspired by this black star's soul music.

TINA TURNER—A CROSSOVER SUCCESS

The career of pop diva Tina Turner is another example of crossover success. Born Anna Mae Bullock on November 26, 1939, in Brownsville, Tennessee, she grew up in the small town of Nut Bush. She began her career in St. Louis, Missouri, in the late 1950s as a rhythm-and-blues and soul singer with bandleader and guitarist Ike Turner. The two eventually married.

The Ike and Tina Turner Revue's first crossover songs included "A Fool in Love" and the Grammy Award–winning "Proud Mary." In 1976, Tina left the abusive Ike and set out on her own. The high-heeled, miniskirted, wild-haired, and leggy singer successfully reshaped her career into one that has gained her international stardom as both recording artist and motion picture actress. Ike and Tina Turner were inducted into the Rock and Roll Hall of Fame in 1991.

JAMES BROWN

(B. 1933)

Called Mr. Dynamite and Soul Brother Number One, and said to have "reinvented soul music at least twice,"[1] this stylish showman influenced American music so heavily over the last half-century that even hip-hop and rap music owe a debt to him.

James Joe Brown Jr.'s birth is made up of the stuff that creates legends. He was born on May 3, 1933 near Barnwell, South Carolina, to Susan Behlings Brown and Joe Brown, a turpentine worker. His birth, however, was a "stillborn" birth: at first, his parents thought he was dead, but his great-aunt Minnie blew breath into his mouth, patted and rubbed him, and he was miraculously brought back to life.

His parents broke up when he was four. His father, who had a mean streak and occasionally beat him, tried to raise him by leaving the little boy alone all night in their shabby cabin out in the woods while he went to work. This experience, wrote Brown in his autobiography *James Brown, The Godfather of Soul,* "worked a change in me that stayed with me from then on. It gave me my own mind. No matter what came my way after that—prison, personal problems,

government harassment—I had the ability to fall back on myself."[2] And he did.

When James was six, he, his father, and his Aunt Minnie moved to nearby Augusta, Georgia, where the child and his aunt moved in with another relative named Handsome "Honey" Washington. His Aunt Honey was said to be able to "read" the hair on people's arms. Whenever she bathed James, she would "go crossways" with the hairs on his little arms, "read" the hairs, and prophesy that he would become a wealthy man one day. And he did.

Aunt Honey's crowded roadhouse on Highway 1 was filled with prostitution, gambling, bootlegging, and fighting. Little James, who quickly learned to defend himself, ran errands, collected coal by the railroad tracks, picked peanuts and cotton, delivered groceries, and danced for nickels and dimes from passing soldiers to help his aunts make ends meet. He "saw everything."

In the streets, he ran into musicians who taught him how to play the drums and guitar, and in church he learned to sing gospel.

He went on to help organize a gospel, then R&B, group called the Flames (later, the Famous Flames) with onetime gospel singer Bobby Byrd. Brown sang and played drums and piano. The Flames released "Please, Please, Please" in 1956, which rocked the R&B charts. In 1962, convinced that he could successfully preserve the fervor of his live performances on an album, Brown used his own money and his backup James Brown Band and rented the Apollo Theater in New York. When Brown's *Live at the Apollo* album was released a year later, it went to an incredible number two listing on *Billboard*'s album chart.

In time he also formed his own forty-member troupe, the James Brown Revue. Brown's intricately choreographed dance steps accompanied the throbbing beat of such songs as "Poppa's Got a Brand New Bag" parts one and two (1965), the rockin' "Ain't That a Groove" (1966), and "Cold Sweat" (1967). His performances caused audiences to jump, shout, gyrate, pass out, and "get down" everywhere.

Having seen his father acquiesce to whites while he was growing up, James Brown vowed to be a strong black man, equal to whites, no matter what. By the late 1960s, Brown had kicked into fifth gear, writing and recording such "black pride" hits as "Don't Be a Dropout" (1966), "Say It Loud: I'm Black and I'm Proud" (1968), "I Don't Want Nobody to Give Me Nothin'" (1969), and other hits that went to the top of the R&B charts.

Because of his pro-black philosophy and his ability to communicate so well with poor black people, Brown helped to boost both Dr. Martin Luther King's civil rights movement as well as the Black Power movement. He was one of the few black leaders who was able to calm down angry black crowds after King was assassinated in 1968.

Brother Brown came back to life again in 1971 with a revamped band called the JBs just in time for the discotheque (disco) crowd. James Brown became the Original Disco Man. The JBs, with trombonist Fred Wesley, saxophonist Maceo Parker, and a young guitarist named Bootsy Collins, produced a new sound called "funk" and another string of hits beginning with "Hot Pants."

Many young adoring performers like Michael Jackson and the Artist Formerly Known as Prince followed Brown's shows, and emulated his every move.

Remembering his poverty-filled childhood, James Brown preaches to young people about the importance of getting a good education, striving to better oneself, and being economically sound by owning businesses. At one time, he owned many businesses, including a real estate agency, a recording studio, and several radio stations.

After the funk and disco thrills of the 1970s faded away, Brown made yet another comeback. He appeared in the movie *The Blues Brothers* (1980). Brown refused to perform in apartheid South Africa. "I might be able to go in and play and cleanse people's nerves, but the sin would continue,"[3] he explained. He also sang the theme song "Living in America" for Sylvester Stallone's movie *Rocky IV* (1985). In

1986, Brown was inducted into the Rock and Roll Hall of Fame and Museum.

In 1992, Brown was given a Grammy Lifetime Achievement Award. Today new generations enjoy this legendary black star's music through the numerous "samplings" of his music on millions of rap and hip-hop records. James Brown, the Godfather of Soul, with over 800 songs in his repertoire, "is universally acknowledged as the most-sampled performer of all time."[4]

✦ When a musician's music is reproduced and used in someone else's recordings, it is called **sampling.**

EXPRESS YOURSELF

The famous Depression-era prophet Daddy Grace and his popular ministerial performances in Augusta, Georgia, inspired James Brown to incorporate portions of what he saw into his own stage performances. Brown's closing show trademark cape idea, however, came to him while he watched wrestler Gorgeous George on television. In Brown's closing routine, he collapses while singing on stage. His assistants drape a cape over his fallen form. They lead the seemingly weakened singer offstage, then to the delight of his screaming audience, Brown casts off the cape, springs back on the stage full of life, and singing his heart out, he brings the house down.

Doug Quimby (b. 1936) Frankie Quimby (b. 1937)

✦

The African and African American slave songs, field hollers, and praise shouts that Georgia Sea Island Singers Doug and Frankie Quimby grew up with as children back in the 1930s and 1940s were the same that their ancestors sang hundreds of years ago.

Frankie Sullivan Quimby was born the oldest of thirteen children on October 5, 1937, in Brunswick, Georgia, and raised on the Georgia Sea Islands. Frankie's ancestors were slaves on the Hopeton and Altama plantations in Glynn County. After the Civil War, they took the name Sullivan. Frankie can trace her family's ancestry back to what is now Nigeria and the Foulah tribe.

Little Frankie loved to play games and sing songs like "All God's Children Got Shoes," "Hambone," and "Wade in the Water" with her friends. But it was not until she met the great singer Bessie Jones when she was fifteen years old that Frankie fully understood the importance of those songs. Most of the songs are in a mixture of English and Gullah words.

Doug Quimby was born on December 23, 1936, in Bacontown,

Georgia, into a family of southwest Georgia sharecroppers. By age four, he was working in the cotton fields. His first paying job came when he was five years old. He would sit in the back of the plantation overseer's truck and sing "My Mother Is Dead and Gone" for the overseer's mother. She would cry the entire way into town and back, then dry her eyes and give him twenty-five cents.[1]

As a teenager, he sang spirituals to himself "out behind the plow."[2] Doug Quimby met Frankie Sullivan on New Year's night in 1964 during a gospel extravaganza at Frankie's church. They married in 1971.

The original Georgia Sea Island Singers were organized in 1921 "to help make sure the Black children know about their heritage."[3]

Frankie and Doug Quimby joined the Georgia Sea Island Singers in 1969. The number of singers diminished over the years. The Quimbys continued to carry on the Georgia Sea Island tradition as a duo.

Slaves had a reason for creating every song and game they sang and played. Most songs were "double-talk." They usually concealed messages about the slave master or how to escape to freedom. Mrs. Quimby said that an elderly man once explained to her husband that the song "All God's Children Got Shoes" was a reminder to the slave master that everybody, even slaves, should have shoes for their feet. "They'd sing, 'Everybody talking about heaven ain't goin',' and then they'd dance and shout and point with their thumbs behind their back or over their shoulders at the slave owners. The slaves were saying, 'and *you* ain't goin'.'"[4]

The song "Hambone" is a traditional slave clapping game in which Doug Quimby rapidly and rhythmically slaps his thighs to beat out the rhythm, as the enslaved did when their "masters" refused to let them play their drums. According to the Quimbys, the words "Hambone, Hambone, where you been? 'Round the world and back again," come from the times when enslaved families would pass from one soup pot to another the leftover hambone off the slave owner's table.

Even today when the Georgia Sea Island Singers perform, "There'll be whites who say, 'I played that game as a child and I didn't know where it came from.'"[5]

Using only the tambourine, clapping hands, feet, audience participation, makeshift instruments like bottles (to make sounds), and their voices, the Quimbys have shared their songs and stories with audiences at Carnegie Hall, the Smithsonian Institution, President Jimmy Carter's Inauguration, the 1994 Winter Olympic Games in Lillehammer, Norway, the 1996 Summer Olympics in Atlanta, and at schools, libraries and festivals around the country, and in Mexico, Canada, Europe, and the continent of Africa. They live in Brunswick, Georgia.

"We tell middle and high school kids to listen to the way the slaves were rapping about what was happening on the plantation," said Mrs. Quimby. "They were doing the same thing that Tupac and Snoop Doggy Dogg are doing, but *they* just blew it out of proportion."[6]

ARETHA FRANKLIN

(B. 1942)

Of all the African American soul singers to gain popularity in the 1960s, none can surpass Aretha Franklin, the Queen of Soul. Rooted in the music of gospel and blues, and born at the edge of this country's most active time of change, Franklin's superb voice, lively rhythms, and timely messages appealed to an entire generation of people who were intent on changing and improving the quality of life for every American.

Aretha Louise Franklin was born on March 25, 1942, in Memphis, Tennessee, home of Beale Street, blues, and composer W. C. Handy. She was the fourth of five children born to Barbara Siggers Franklin and the Reverend Clarence Franklin. The family moved to Detroit when Aretha was a toddler.

Her mother was a talented gospel singer, and her father was pastor of Detroit's New Bethel Baptist Church. Rev. Franklin was popular in the National Baptist Convention, and his personality and lively sermons drew people from all over to his church. Aretha's mother died when Aretha was ten years old.

Aretha and her siblings grew up singing foot-stomping gospel in New Bethel Baptist Church. She and her sisters Erma and Carolyn often sang gospel together as children, and when they were adults, they sang together as the Franklin Sisters. Her brother Cecil became a minister. Rev. Franklin carefully directed Aretha's musical career while she was growing up.

Professional musicians were frequent visitors to the Franklin home. Little Aretha always enjoyed the many talented people around her, such as Mahalia Jackson. She remembers that it was Clara Ward who inspired her as a singer. The Reverend James Cleveland, legendary gravelly voiced minister and vocalist, taught Aretha to play the piano just like he did. Gospel-singer-turned-rhythm-and-blues-celebrity Sam Cooke was also a close friend.

Although Aretha grew up solidly based in the church, she listened to Detroit's up-and-coming Motown singers and groups. She also heard popular 1950s rhythm-and-blues (R&B) doo-wop artists such as the Platters, the Drifters, the Clovers, Frankie Lymon and the Teenagers, the Flamingos, Little Anthony and the Imperials, Lloyd Price, Jackie Wilson, Ruth Brown, Little Richard, Chuck Berry, Fats Domino, B. B. King, and the Coasters.

✦ **Doo-wop** is a style of 1950s urban music in which small groups of vocalists would harmonize songs, making up nonsense words for the rhythms, like doo-wop, de-wop, bamma-lamma-lamma dingdong, and shoo-shoo be-doo.

As a child, Aretha was a popular gospel singer. She started working as a soloist in her father's Baptist choir during revivals, and traveled with him around the country. When she was only fourteen, she recorded her first album. By the time she was seventeen, Aretha was a single mother, but she received positive support from her close-knit family. When she turned eighteen, Aretha and her father decided it was time to take her career to the next level.

Aretha moved to New York in 1960 and signed with Columbia

Records. She recorded several albums with Columbia, but she wanted to sing blues and gospel. In 1966, she signed with Atlantic Records, which had a history of successfully promoting black vocalists. This was a major turning point in Aretha's career. She could now play and sing rhythm and blues in her own bluesy, gospel way.

Her first record on the Atlantic label, "I Ain't Never Loved a Man (the Way I Love You)," sold a quarter of a million copies in its first fourteen days. Another song released from the same album was "Respect," written by the great Otis Redding.

When "Respect" was released in 1967, it "blew the top off the charts."[1] She followed it up with "You Make Me Feel Like a Natural Woman" and "Think." The messages in these songs electrified the imagination of people who were struggling for equality among the races, for equality between the sexes, and to end the Vietnam War.

In 1967, American society was filled with turmoil. In some black neighborhoods, the summer of 1967 was known as "the summer of 'Retha, rap, and revolt."[2] Her song "Respect" went gold. It would be the first of many. Aretha was now being hailed as the Queen of Soul.

Aretha's personal life has been filled with the heartaches and the blues she expresses in her songs. Her first marriage was unhappy and ended in divorce. Her second marriage, to actor Glenn Turman of *Cooley High* movie fame, also ended. Her father was shot during a robbery at his home in 1979 and died in 1984. Her younger sister, Carolyn, who collaborated with her on a number of her albums, died of cancer in 1988. In 1990, her brother, the Reverend Cecil Franklin, died of a heart attack. She sang at the funerals of her dear friends the Reverend Doctor Martin Luther King Jr. and Mahalia Jackson.

Despite her heartaches and tragedies, Aretha Franklin, now the mother of four sons, continues her triumphs. In 1980, Aretha left Atlantic Records and signed with Arista, where she continued to produce successful records. She has sung for U.S. presidents at the White House on many occasions. She has received the prestigious Kennedy

Center Honors Award, and was the first woman to be inducted into the Rock and Roll Hall of Fame. She received both a Grammy Legends Award and a Grammy Lifetime Achievement Award. She was also featured in the 1980 smash movie *Blues Brothers* and in its sequel, *Blues Brothers 2000.* She has won more Grammies than any other woman, and in 1999 released her first autobiography.

Her 1998 album *A Rose Is Still a Rose* was a best-seller. Aretha Franklin, the Queen of Soul, is getting a round of "respect" from a whole new generation of listeners.

LAURYN HILL—THE NEXT GENERATION

Lauryn Hill, previously of the Fugees, is the first woman to win five Grammy awards at one time, including album of the year for *The Mis-education of Lauryn Hill.* The young singer first found fame in Whoopi Goldberg's movie *Sister Act 2.* Like Aretha Franklin, Hill has set new standards in her field by working to merge rap and hip-hop with the classic soul music she grew up with. Also like Franklin, Hill is a songwriter, arranger, and producer. With rapper and music executive Sean "Puffy" Combs, she helped write, arrange, and produce Aretha Franklin's hit album *A Rose Is Still a Rose.*

JESSYE NORMAN

(B. 1945)

Jessye Norman began to sing when she was two years old. By the time she was five, she was singing in the children's choir at Mount Calvary Baptist Church in her hometown of Augusta, Georgia. From this early beginning in her neighborhood church, Jessye Norman would build a most successful career in the world of classical music.

Jessye Norman was born into a prosperous, middle-class family in Augusta's tight-knit black community of Bethlehem on September 15, 1945. She was the second oldest of five children. Her father, Silas Norman, was a Sunday school superintendent at Mount Calvary Baptist and a salesman for North Carolina Mutual Insurance. Her mother, Jane Norman, was a local church auditor and a secretary for the Democratic Party. Both parents were actively involved in Augusta and encouraged and supported their children's activities.

All of the Norman children learned to play the piano. According to Mrs. Norman, Jessye loved listening to the radio while she did her housework, and was always thrilled to hear the voice of the magnificent contralto Marian Anderson.

Jessye attended C. T. Walker Elementary School, A. R. Johnson Junior High, and Lucy Laney High School, all segregated schools. Her first performance for an audience was at C. T. Walker Elementary when she sang "Mary, Mary, Quite Contrary, How Does Your Garden Grow?" She entered her first singing competition at Mount Calvary when she was seven, and won third place. The church and choir were very important parts of Jessye's upbringing. She told *Augusta* magazine, "We learned a great deal about life and living" by being in Mount Calvary's choirs. "We learned how to behave towards one another in a group setting, and how to allow more than one person to 'have the lead' in a song, all those important lessons that last a lifetime."[1]

By seventh grade, Jessye was already 5 feet 7 inches tall and her music teachers had discovered her exceptional voice. But she also had a weight problem. When she walked out onto the stage, children laughed at her because she was "so big," according to Rosa Sanders Creque, her A. R. Johnson music teacher. "But when she sang, they got very still."[2] Although Jessye had a magnificent voice, many thought that her race and her weight would limit her chances of becoming a successful classical singer. Knowing that she had the support and respect of her family and community, and having "very positive information about [her] own self-worth,"[3] she refused to be restricted by racial prejudice. Instead, she began singing more at churches, recreation centers, schools, Girl Scout programs, PTAs, and even supermarket openings. She entered her first national competition at an Omega Psi Phi program in Philadelphia, where she won third place.

Her next major competition was the Marian Anderson Scholarship competition in Philadelphia when she was sixteen. Although she didn't win, the trip gave her the opportunity to stop in Washington, D.C., and audition for music professor Dr. Carolyn Grant at Howard University. The school immediately offered her a music scholarship. Since Jessye was too young to accept the scholarship, the university held it for her until she graduated from high school and enrolled at Howard.

After receiving her bachelor's degree in music with honors from Howard University in 1967, she went to the Peabody Conservatory of Music in Baltimore, Maryland, and then to the University of Michigan at Ann Arbor, where she studied with Pierre Bernac and received her master's degree in 1968. Norman also traveled throughout South America in 1968 as a member of the U.S. State Department's People-to-People tour.

A scholarship from the Institute of International Education that same year allowed her to take her first trip to Europe, where she won first prize in an International Music Competition sponsored by Germany's Munich Radio. In 1969, after winning several more competitions, Jessye Norman moved to Berlin, where she appeared with the Deutsche Oper Berlin as principal soprano. She also debuted as Elisabeth in Wagner's opera *Tannhäuser* to enthusiastic reviews. Like Marian Anderson, Roland Hayes, Elizabeth Taylor Greenfield, and many other African American classical singers, Norman had found a receptive audience in Europe.

In 1972, she made her professional debut in the United States in the opera *Aïda* at the Hollywood Bowl in Los Angeles, and at Lincoln Center in New York the following year. In 1983, she performed at the Metropolitan Opera House at its one-hundredth-anniversary production of Berlioz's opera *The Trojans,* with tenor Plácido Domingo. Fluent in German, French, Italian, Spanish, Hebrew, and Latin, she has sung many of the world's most famous operas, accompanied by the major orchestras of the world.

Jessye Norman's awards include a number of Grammies, London's prestigious Gramophone Award, and the Paris *Grand Prix National du Disque* award. She has received the Investiture of *Commandeur de l'Ordre des Arts et des Lettres* from the French government, and was presented with the *Légion d'Honneur* by France's President Mitterrand.

Leontyne Price takes a curtain call at the end of a performance of Giuseppe Verdi's famous opera Aïda.

LEONTYNE PRICE—CLASSICAL DIVA

The first African American classical singer to be truly called a Metropolitan Opera star was Leontyne Price. She was born Mary Violet Leontine (later changed to Leontyne) Price on February 10, 1927, in Laurel, Mississippi. She was the daughter of James and Kate Price. After hearing Marian Anderson sing in a concert, young Leontine, who sang in her church choir and played piano, decided she, too, would have a career in music.

Ms. Price's breakthrough singing role was as Bess in George Gershwin's landmark folk opera *Porgy and Bess.* She toured with the opera in Europe from 1952 to 1954. After her concert debut as a soprano in November 1954 at Town Hall, her career ascended rapidly. Her historic debut at the Metropolitan Opera came in January 1961 in Verdi's opera *Il Trovatore.* For her performance, the audience gave her a forty-two-minute ovation, the longest ever given at the Met at that time.

One of the most unusual distinctions she has received is having an orchid named for her by the National Museum of Natural History in Paris.

She has been an honorary ambassador to the United Nations and has received honorary doctorates from nearly thirty colleges, universities, and conservatories around the world, including Howard University, Harvard, Yale, Cambridge, the Juilliard School of Music, and Augusta's Paine College.

In a 1982 *Newsweek* magazine article, Annalyn Swan wrote, "Everything about Jessye Norman is larger than life—her size, her voice and her vibrant personality. . . . On an opera stage, her eyes flash, her head arches high and she moves with the inexorable surge of a ship at sea."[4]

As one of the most famous opera stars currently performing, Norman is well aware of the racism her African American predecessors faced. She has said, "I'm grateful to Marian Anderson, Dorothy Maynor, Leontyne Price, and all the rest for having paved the way. . . . Look, it's unrealistic to pretend that racial prejudice doesn't exist. It does! It's one thing to have a set of laws, and quite another to change the hearts and minds of men."[5]

Jessye Norman has sung for U.S. presidents from Lyndon B. Johnson to Bill Clinton. On April 16, 1996, Augusta's riverwalk amphitheater was named the Jessye Norman Amphitheater and Plaza. Although she maintains a home in upstate New York and another in London, she keeps close ties with Augusta. When she is not traveling or working, she is busy with civic and humanitarian causes such as the Dance Theater of Harlem and the Girl Scouts of America.

STEVIE WONDER

(B. 1950)

The emergence of soul and rock-and-roll music turned the late 1950s and the 1960s into a golden age for black music. Black artists were finally being recognized, and their music could be heard on both white and black radio stations. By the end of the 1960s, black music was finally recognized as a major part of American music.

In the 1970s, discotheque dance music came along. It was based on computerized keyboard arrangements that kept a steady, energetic beat. James Brown called himself the Original Disco Man, and Donna Summer earned the title of Queen of Disco when she fused the psychedelic beat to her soulful sounds. This also was the music of a young harmonica-and-drums-playing youngster from Michigan named Little Stevie Wonder.

Stevland Judkins Morris was born prematurely on May 13, 1950, in Saginaw, Michigan, to Lula Morris. An accident at the hospital—the wrong amount of oxygen in his incubator— caused scar tissue to grow behind his eyeballs. This caused him to lose his sight.

The family moved to Detroit, where Stevie grew up in the

Whitestone Baptist Church Choir. He learned to play the piano, drums, organ, and harmonica, and by age eleven was considered a child prodigy. Stevie's musical career took a big leap forward when he was introduced to Motown (then called Hitsville USA) Recording Company producer Berry Gordy. Stevie was signed to Motown at age eleven, and Gordy gave him the stage name "Little Stevie" Wonder.

Little Stevie's first hit was "Fingertips Part 2." He played the harmonica, and recorded the song live at the Regal Theater in Chicago. It became the "first live single ever" to hit number one on the *Billboard* charts. Stevie's great uncle, Walter Morris, adopted him, and Gordy enrolled Stevie in classes at the Michigan School for the Blind.

By the mid-1960s, Stevie Wonder had dropped "Little" from his name and had recorded such hit songs as "My Cherie Amour," "Uptight," "I Was Made to Love Her," and "For Once in My Life." He also found himself at the White House receiving a Distinguished Service Award from President Richard Nixon's Committee on the Employment of Handicapped People. In 1969, he released an album under the name Eivets Rednow, his name spelled backward.

In the 1970s, Stevie married singer Syreeta Wright, but they soon divorced. He also wrested control of his music career from Motown in 1971 and created his own publishing company, Black Bull Music.

Wonder, who has won Grammies by the handfuls throughout his career, is hailed as a trailblazer because of his ability to create different kinds of music and play a variety of instruments. He was among the first African Americans to use electronic music in their work. On his 1972 album *Talking Book,* he played all the instruments and sang all the vocals. He is also credited with being one of the first to use the synthesizer in musical arrangements.

Wonder's numerous public service messages and contributions to worthy causes such as the Charge Against Hunger campaign and Mothers Against Drunk Driving have endeared him to many. Along with superstars Michael Jackson, Quincy Jones, and a list of popular singers, he helped create the 1985 album *We Are the World,* which helped feed the hungry in Ethiopia and the United States. He joined Dionne Warwick in her 1986 *That's What Friends Are For* album to help AIDS victims. He has sung against South Africa's racist apartheid regime, and continues his efforts to help blind and other handicapped people.

Stevie Wonder was part of the nationwide drive to make the Reverend Doctor Martin Luther King Jr.'s birthday in January a national holiday. U.S. House of Representatives congressman John Conyers proposed the legislation just four days after King was murdered. Wonder released his album *Hotter Than July* in 1979. It included his "Happy Birthday" tribute to Dr. King.

After some 6 million names were gathered on petitions and submitted to Congress, and after marches, arrests, and intense lobbying, President Ronald Reagan passed legislation that made Dr. King's birthday observed as a federal holiday.

Stevie Wonder recently appeared in actor and rapper Will Smith's *Wild, Wild West* music video from the blockbuster movie of the same name. He was inducted into the Rock and Roll Hall of Fame in 1989.

Berry Gordy and the Motown Sound

Berry Gordy, a Detroit songwriter, was an assembly-line worker who loved jazz. He opened a record store in 1955. His song "Lonely Teardrops" was recorded by singer Jackie Wilson in 1958 and became a hit. With $800, Gordy started his own musical company in 1959 and called it Hitsville USA. He later changed it to Motown, which was part of Detroit's nickname.

The first group Gordy recorded was Smokey Robinson and the Miracles. Other groups and solo artists, including Martha and the Vandellas, the Marvelettes, the Supremes, the Jackson Five, Michael Jackson, Marvin Gaye, the Temptations, the Four Tops, Gladys Knight and the Pips, and Stevie Wonder, soon followed. Gordy sold Motown on June 29, 1988, to MCA for $61 million.

Michael Jackson

(B. 1958)

Michael Joe Jackson was born August 29, 1958, in Gary, Indiana, the fifth of nine children born to Joseph and Katherine Scruse Jackson. Katherine Jackson suffered from polio as a child and wore braces until high school. Although she recovered from the disease, she always walked with a limp. She worked part-time at Sears, played the guitar, and loved country music. Joseph Jackson was a crane operator, foundry worker, and former blues guitarist. When money was low, he worked many odd jobs to make ends meet. Both parents were strict traditionalists and believed in physically disciplining their children.

Because the Jacksons lived in a "rough and often dangerous" neighborhood, Mrs. Jackson, who was a devout Jehovah's Witness, did not allow the children to play in the streets with other children.[1] The family was poor, but they were never impoverished.

The boys used to listen to their father practice his guitar with his former blues band. They longed to play, too, but he had warned them not to play with his guitar. When their father was gone, nine-year-old

Jackie, seven-year-old Tito, and six-year-old Jermaine would sneak out the guitar and play it.

Once their mother caught them. Instead of punishing them, Mrs. Jackson, who loved country-and-western music, played the music on her guitar and taught the boys to sing along. Eventually, Tito broke a guitar string. When Mr. Jackson found out, he punished Tito. But later that night he asked Tito to play the guitar and was amazed at how good he was. The next day Mr. Jackson came home with a red electric guitar and gave it to Tito. He called the three boys together to hear them sing and play. This was the beginning of what would eventually be the Jackson Five.

The group would soon include little Michael. As a toddler, Michael "would hold his bottle and dance to the rhythm of the washing machine."[2] His first public solo performance was when he was five years old. The energetic, confident little boy sang "Climb Ev'ry Mountain" at his elementary school and received a standing ovation.

Mr. Jackson, who had visions of musical greatness for his children, entered the boys in a talent contest, which they won. After winning more local talent contests, they entered a contest at Chicago's Regal Theater and won first place. By now, Michael was eight years old and singing lead vocals. Tito was on guitar, Jermaine on bass guitar, Jackie on shakers, and a friend of the family, Johnny Jackson, was on drums.

They became the opening act throughout the Northeast for rhythm-and-blues, soul, and pop acts such as Gladys Knight and the Pips, the Temptations, Etta James, Joe Simon, and James Brown. Michael demonstrated so much dance originality that he became the group's choreographer. As a young performer, Michael Jackson was very much influenced by James Brown. Brown even showed Michael "how to drop the mike and then catch it before it hit the stage floor."[3]

Soon, the Jackson family caught the attention of singers Gladys Knight and Bobby Taylor, who brought the group to the attention of Motown founder Berry Gordy. He quickly signed the group to the label.

The Jackson Five's first hit on the Motown label, which by now had moved from Detroit to Los Angeles, was "I Want You Back" in 1969. The next year, the song went to number one on the pop and rhythm-and-blues charts. A number of top-twenty singles, including "ABC," "Never Can Say Goodbye," "Little Bitty Pretty One," and "Dancing Machine," followed. The Jackson Five were soaring up the charts, and in the mid-1970s, practically everyone was dancing to the Jackson beat.

Eager to write and produce their own material, the Jackson Five left Motown and signed with Epic in 1976. Now known simply as The Jacksons, they kept on making hits like "Blame It on the Boogie," "Shake Your Body," "Lovely One," and "Heartbreak Hotel" on the Epic label.

By this time, lead singer Michael had become more popular than his brothers. After starring with Diana Ross in the movie classic *The Wiz,* he began working with arranger Quincy Jones on a solo album—*Off the Wall.* The album was released in 1979 and produced such hits as "Don't Stop Till You Get Enough," "Rock with You," "Off the Wall," and "She's Outta My Life." He also co-wrote the hit single "The Girl Is Mine" with former Beatle Paul McCartney in 1982.

In 1982, he released his second solo album, the gigantic, record-setting, hit-producing *Thriller.* It spent thirty-seven weeks on the U.S. charts, and is the best-selling album in U.S. history. It produced seven top-ten hits, was awarded eight Grammies, and was entered into the Guinness Book of Records. Jackson initiated the "moonwalk" dance craze and started wearing a rhinestoned glove on one hand.

In 1984, the soft-spoken singer received a presidential award from Ronald Reagan. He supports numerous projects to help underprivileged children in the United States and elsewhere. And he helped produce the *We Are the World* album, which he co-wrote with Lionel Richie, to aid famine relief in Africa and the United States.

Michael Jackson became the single most successful entertainer in the twentieth century, amassing Grammies and American Music

DIANA ROSS: FROM BACKUP SINGER TO STAR

Diane Ernestine Ross was born on March 26, 1944, in Detroit. She is the daughter of Fred and Ernestine Ross. On her birth certificate, however, her name was written Diana. The family still calls her Diane.[4] This thin young girl with the big eyes, wide mouth, perky voice, and abundant ambition would one day leave the projects and, along with Michael Jackson, become one of the biggest black stars of the 1960s, 1970s, and 1980s.

Her singing career began with her friends Mary Wilson, Florence Ballard, and Barbara Martin. They called themselves the Primettes. The fledgling group signed with the Motown Recording Company in 1961. Berry Gordy, Motown's owner, changed the group's name to the Supremes. Martin left the group, and the trio started singing as backups and fill-ins for Gordy's more popular Motown stars until their first big hit, "Where Did Our Love Go?" was released in June 1964. Gordy saw Ross's star potential and guided her career.

In 1967, the group's name was changed to Diana Ross and the Supremes. Ballard was dropped from the group and replaced by Cindy Birdsong. Birdsong was a former singer with songstress Patti LaBelle and the Blue-Belles. Florence Ballard fell into poverty, and she died in 1976.

Between 1965 and 1969, the Motown trio garnered twelve number-one hits. Their fans included teens and adults around the world. After the Supremes' last hit, "Someday We'll Be Together," Diana Ross left the group. In 1970 she established a solo career with "Ain't No Mountain High Enough," written by Motown husband-and-wife songwriters Nick Ashford and Valerie Simpson. A string of hits, including "Touch Me in the Morning" (1975), followed. Ross left Motown in 1981 to pursue an even larger singing career with other record companies.

Ross has established herself not only as a top entertainment icon but also as an actress, starring as the legendary Billie Holiday in *Lady Sings the Blues* (1972), for which she was nominated for an Oscar, and also in *Mahogany* (1975) and the popular *The Wiz* (1978). In 1988, Diana Ross and the Supremes were inducted into the Rock and Roll Hall of Fame.

Diana Ross moved into television production and produced several made-for-TV movies. Ross continues to be a popular entertainer who is now best known for her reminiscent albums and her live concerts in New York's Central Park. In 1999, she starred with young singer and actress Brandy in the ABC Television movie *Double Platinum*. They were both executive producers of the movie.

Awards for practically every pop and R&B category. He has received NAACP, *Essence,* and *Ebony* magazine honors, MTV video awards, and worldwide recognition. In 1993, he received a Grammy Legend Award, and in 1997, as part of the Jacksons, he was inducted into the Rock and Roll Hall of Fame.

Most of his brothers produced albums as well, and his sisters LaToya and Maureen (Rebbie) each made an album. His baby sister Janet has become a successful Grammy-winning singer, dancer, and actress.

In 1994, Jackson married Lisa Marie Presley, daughter of rock-and-roll legend Elvis Presley, but they soon divorced. Jackson remarried, was divorced again, and is now the father of two children. The resourceful, eccentric, and imaginative shining star has always been known for his creative originality. The future holds what happens next.

QUEEN LATIFAH

(B. 1970)

Queen Latifah was born Dana Elaine Owens on March 18, 1970, in Newark, New Jersey. Her parents were Rita and Lancelot Owens, who was a policeman. She began singing at Shiloh Baptist Church in Bloomfield, New Jersey. When Dana was seven, her parents separated. Her mother moved Dana and her older brother, Lance Jr., nicknamed Winki, out of their comfortable middle-class apartment into a low-income housing project.

To make ends meet, Mrs. Owens worked at the post office, waited tables at the Newark Airport, and took college classes to get the education that she had postponed when she married. Little Dana admired her mother for her energy, her dignity, and her ability to overcome obstacles. This same energy, dedication, and self-pride carried over into Dana and helped her to become a Grammy Award–winning rap star, record company CEO, and actress.

When Dana was eight, she was physically big for her age. She loved to climb trees, play basketball and baseball, and beat up boys. One day she and her cousin Sharonda decided to give themselves

Muslim names. Many adults and friends around them were doing the same thing, because black pride was still strong in the black community.

They looked through a book of Muslim names. Sharonda picked out a name. They made up a song using Sharonda's Muslim name. Dana picked out Latifah because it meant "delicate, sensitive, kind."[1] She thought it described who she really was inside.

About the same time that Dana chose Latifah for a new name, an equally new, urban music style called "rap" was being created in nearby New York City. According to Nelson George in his book *The Death of Rhythm and Blues,* computerized white disco of the 1970s replaced traditional soul, funk, and pop music on New York urban black radio airwaves. This wasn't what young inner-city black youth wanted to hear. Instead, they made up their own rhymes, slogans, and phrases, and played music not heard on the radio.

The first rap song to gain national attention was "Rapper's Delight" (1979) by the Sugar Hill Gang. This was the kind of rap music that young Dana and her friends also heard and loved. She loved rap so much that by the time she was a teenager, she would slip over to New York City to the Latin Quarter to be with other teenagers who loved it, too. And then she'd bring back the songs, the dances, and the clothing styles to her friends in her neighborhood after the family moved to East Orange, New Jersey, and to Irvington High School, where she was a student.

She first learned how to "freestyle"—make and tape her own rhymes over music mixes—in the basement of DJ Mark James, who hosted dances at Latifah's school. Sometimes she was the only girl there in a crowd of boys. "I called myself Princess of the Posse," Queen Latifah wrote in her book *Ladies First: Revelations of a Strong Woman.* "It was like being in rap school. . . . Our goal then wasn't to get a record deal; it was to become good."[2]

When not in school or in Mark's basement, Dana was working at Burger King. During high school, she formed the rap group Ladies

Fresh and also played on the school's girl's basketball team. The team won two state championships while she was a player. After graduation, she attended Borough of Manhattan Community College for a semester, then dropped out to pursue rap music and the entertainment field. Her "Princess of the Posse" rap demo opened doors. In 1988, on the Tommy Boy label, she released her first single, "Wrath of My Madness." Like Ella Fitzgerald and Sarah Vaughan, Latifah made a successful appearance at the Apollo Theater.

Her first album, *All Hail the Queen,* was released in 1989 and was nominated for a Grammy. About this time she added "Queen" to her childhood name of Latifah as a tribute to great African queens. "Queen became synonymous with woman for me," she explained, "the way every woman should feel or should want to feel."[3]

As Queen Latifah's career grew, she wisely invested part of her finances into a delicatessen and a video store near where she lived. In 1991, she created Flavor Unit Records and Management Company in Jersey City, New Jersey. But tragedy came into her life when her brother Winki was killed in a motorcycle accident on April 26, 1992. Devastated by the loss, Latifah dedicated the song "Winki's Theme" to him on her album *Black Reign* on the Motown label in 1993.

Her song "U.N.I.T.Y." received a Grammy in 1995. This talented black star has also found a niche in television and movies. Her most famous role to date was as Cleo in the movie *Set It Off.* She also was featured in *Juice, Jungle Fever,* and *House Party II.* Most TV fans know Queen Latifah from her successful TV comedy series *Living Single.*

Queen Latifah has released records and videos that uplift young women, criticize drug use, and rarely include curse words. She remains concerned about the sexist, negative images of women being described in some rap songs and videos.

Today rap and its hip-hop culture have attracted so many young people that it has spawned an international, multibillion-dollar music and merchandising industry.

Hip-hop music has brought riches to labels such as Death Row Records, Def Jam Recordings, and Bad Boy Recordings, and to individual rappers and groups such as Snoop Dogg, Run DMC, Kool Mo Dee, Public Enemy, Ice T, Biggie Smalls (The Notorious B.I.G.), Busta Rhymes, LL Kool J, Dr. Dre, Sean "Puffy" Combs, and Tupac Shakur.

TUPAC SHAKUR—A FALLEN STAR

Rapper, actor, and songwriter Tupac (2Pak) Shakur was born on June 16, 1971, in New York City. Tupac had his first acting role at age twelve, when he played the part of Travis in Lorraine Hansberry's play *Raisin in the Sun*. He wrote his first rap song under the name of MC New York while he attended the Baltimore School of Arts in Baltimore, Maryland. He made his first album *2Pacalypse Now* in 1991. He appeared in the films *Juice* (1992), *Poetic Justice* (with Janet Jackson in 1993), and *Above the Rim* (1994).

Tupac's best-selling album *Me Against the World* produced the poignant single "Dear Mama" and spent many weeks at number one on the *Billboard* charts. Despite his many platinum-selling albums and movie roles and his international celebrity status, Tupac openly lived what he said was a "thug's life." He was involved in at least two shooting incidents. The first nearly took his life, and the last—on September 7, 1996, in Las Vegas—was fatal. Tupac Shakur died on September 13, 1996, at age twenty-five.

Female rappers have had a harder time than men breaking through, but girl rapper groups Salt-N-Pepa, divas Lauryn Hill and Mary J. Blige, and singers/songwriters/producers Missy Elliott and Queen Latifah have created enduring names for themselves.

CHRONOLOGY

1809	Concert singer Elizabeth Taylor Greenfield born.
1827	Composer and violinist Edmund Dede born.
1849	Pianist Thomas "Blind Tom" Greene Bethune born.
	Harriet Tubman escapes from slavery in Maryland. Tubman, called the Moses of enslaved African Americans, would free more than 300 slaves. Songs and drums were often used to help guide escaped slaves to the North.
1851	Millie-Christine McCoy, musical Siamese twins, born.
	Concert singer Elizabeth Taylor Greenfield debuts with Buffalo (N.Y.) Music Association.
1861	Civil War begins when Confederates attack Fort Sumter, South Carolina.
1865	Civil War ends.
1866	Race riot kills nearly fifty people in Memphis, Tennessee, which would become a center for the blues.
	Race riot kills thirty-five in New Orleans, which would become a center for jazz, brass bands, and swing.
	Fisk University opens in Nashville, Tennessee, and soon becomes known for its Fisk Jubilee Singers.
1868	Scott Joplin, the King of Ragtime, born.
1871	Fisk Jubilee Singers take first tour in the United States and Europe.
1873	William C. Handy, Father of the Blues, born.
1876	Elizabeth Taylor Greenfield dies.
1883	Eubie Blake, composer and pianist, born.
1886	Gertrude "Ma" Rainey, the Mother of the Blues, born.
1887	Concert singer Roland Hayes born.
1888	Choir director, arranger, and composer Francis Hall Johnson born.
1889	Noble Sissle, lyricist, born.
1894	Edmund Thornton Jenkins, classical composer, born.
	Bessie Smith born.
1896	First coin-operated electric piano, the Tonophon, hits the market, paving way for first jukeboxes.
	U.S. Supreme Court ruling on Louisiana transportation lawsuit *Plessy* v. *Ferguson* that "separate but equal" facilities for African Americans and whites is constitutional. Ruling bans African Americans, including musicians, from traveling with whites in the same railroad, eating and lodging facilities.

1897	Marian Anderson, concert singer, born.
1898	Paul Robeson, concert singer, actor, athlete, and activist, born.
1899	Edward Kennedy "Duke" Ellington born.
	Thomas Andrew Dorsey, the Father of Modern Gospel Music, born.
1901	Louis Armstrong born.
1903	Edmund Dede dies.
1904	William (Bill) "Count" Basie, jazz pianist and bandleader, born.
1908	Thomas "Blind Tom" Greene Bethune dies.
1912	Millie-Christine McCoy, celebrated singing Siamese twins, die.
	Mahalia Jackson, gospel singer, born.
	W. C. Handy publishes "Memphis Blues."
1914	W. C. Handy completes "St. Louis Blues."
1915	Billie Holiday—"Lady Day"—born.
	Blues artist Muddy Waters born.
1917	Scott Joplin dies.
	United States enters World War I. African American musicians, including composer James Reese Europe, enter the military.
	Ella Fitzgerald, First Lady of Song, born.
1918	World War I ends. Pace & Handy Publishers move to New York with a new hit, "A Good Man Is Hard to Find."
1919	Nat "King" Cole, jazz pianist and singer, born.
1920	Saxophonist Charlie Parker born.
1921	Nobel Sissle and Eubie Blake's *Shuffle Along* opens at the Sixty-third Street Theater in New York.
1923	Bessie Smith records "Down-Hearted Blues," which sells nearly a million copies.
1924	Noble Sissle and Eubie Blake open the musical *Chocolate Dandies.*
	Roland Hayes named soloist with the Boston Symphony Orchestra and awarded NAACP's Spingarn Medal.
1925	Riley "B. B." King, King of the Blues, born.
	Marian Anderson appears in concert with the New York Philharmonic at the Lewisohn Stadium.
1926	Edmund Thornton Jenkins, classical composer, dies.
	Chuck Berry, King of Rock and Roll, born.
1927	Leontyne Price, opera singer, born.
1929	Berry Gordy Jr., promoter and record producer, born.
	Ray Charles Robinson, R&B singer, born.

1931 Composer William Grant Still's *Afro-American Symphony* performed by Rochester Philharmonic Symphony.

1932 James Cleveland, King of Gospel, born.

Franklin D. Roosevelt elected president. His wife, Eleanor Roosevelt, would support Marian Anderson's right to sing at Constitution Hall in Washington, D.C.

1933 Hall Johnson's folk drama *Run Little Chillun* opens on Broadway.

James Joe Brown Jr., Godfather of Soul, born.

Quincy Delight Jones, composer, born.

Wilmington, North Carolina, native Caterina Jarboro sings *Aïda* with Chicago Civic Opera, becoming first black woman to perform in a leading role with an American opera company.

1934 Ella Fitzgerald wins first place at the Apollo Theater in New York.

Imitation of Life opens with Louise Beavers and Claudette Colbert, featuring gospel singer Mahalia Jackson.

1935 George Gershwin writes folk opera *Porgy and Bess.*

Richard "Little Richard" Wayne Penniman, Tutti-Frutti King, born.

1936 Doug Quimby born.

1937 Blues singer Bessie Smith dies.

Frankie Quimby born.

1939 Singer Tina Turner born.

Gertrude "Ma" Rainey, Mother of the Blues, dies.

Marian Anderson refused permission by Daughters of the American Revolution to sing at Washington, D.C.'s Constitution Hall.

1942 Aretha Franklin born.

Soul singer and songwriter Curtis ("Keep On Pushin'") Mayfield born.

1945 Jessye Norman, concert singer, born.

1947 Freedom Riders from the organization Congress of Racial Equality (CORE) test the 1946 ban against segregation in interstate bus travel. Another wave of freedom rides in 1961 opens the way for African Americans, including musicians, to travel on integrated buses and trains throughout the South.

1950 Stevland Morris (Stevie) Wonder, singer and composer, born.

1954 U.S. Supreme Court rules in *Brown* v. *Board of Education* that separate educational facilities are unconstitutional.

1955	Chuck Berry's first big hit record, "Maybellene," is released.
	Marian Anderson becomes the first African American to sing at the Metropolitan Opera.
	Mahalia Jackson meets the Reverend Martin Luther King Jr. in Denver, Colorado, during National Baptist Convention.
1958	Michael Jackson, the King of Pop, born.
	W. C. Handy dies.
1959	Billie Holiday dies.
1960	Prince Rogers Nelson, a.k.a. Prince, a.k.a. the Artist Formerly Known as Prince, rock star and composer, born.
	Greensboro, North Carolina, lunch counter sit-ins and Ray Charles's "What I Say" usher in soul music, the civil rights movement, and the '60s.
1961	President John F. Kennedy inaugurated. Marian Anderson and Mahalia Jackson sing at gala ceremonies.
1965	Black Muslim leader Malcolm X assassinated in New York.
1970	Francis Hall Johnson dies.
	Queen Latifah born.
1971	Louis Armstrong dies.
	Tupac Shakur, rap star, born.
1972	Mahalia Jackson dies.
1974	Duke Ellington dies.
1976	Paul Robeson dies.
1978	William Grant Still dies.
1979	The Sugar Hill Gang produce landmark rap single, "Rapper's Delight."
1982	Composer Quincy Jones and Michael Jackson produce record-breaking "Thriller" album.
1983	Rap song "The Message" released by Grandmaster Flash and the Furious Five.
1986	Dr. Martin Luther King's birthday becomes a federal holiday.
1987	Ella Fitzgerald receives the National Medal of Arts from President Reagan.
1993	Reverend Thomas Andrew Dorsey, Father of Gospel Music, dies.
1996	Ella Fitzgerald dies.
	Tupac Shakur dies.
2000	"Lift Ev'ry Voice and Sing," written in 1900 by James Weldon Johnson with music by his brother J. Rosamond Johnson—and often called the "black national anthem"—celebrates its one hundredth birthday.

NOTES

INTRODUCTION

1. Gwendolin Sims Warren, *Ev'ry Time I Feel the Spirit* (New York: Henry Holt and Company, 1997), 15.
2. Ibid.
3. Ibid.

ELIZABETH TAYLOR GREENFIELD

1. Jessie Carney Smith, ed., *Notable Black American Women* (Detroit: Gale Research, Inc., 1992), 412.
2. Ibid., 413.
3. Arthur R. LaBrew, *Elizabeth T. Greenfield*, 2 vols. (Detroit: Privately printed, 1969–1984), 414.

EDMUND DEDE

1. Lester Sullivan, "Composers of Nineteenth-Century New Orleans: The History Behind the Music," *Black Music Research Journal* 8, no. 1 (1988): 59–60.
2. Maud Cuney-Hare, *Negro Musicians and Their Music* (Washington, D.C.: Associated Publishers, Inc., 1936), 237.

THOMAS "BLIND TOM" GREENE BETHUNE

1. James Haskins, *Black Music in America: A History Through Its People.* (1987; reprint, New York: HarperTrophy Edition, 1993), 15.

MILLIE-CHRISTINE MCCOY

1. William S. Powell, ed., *Dictionary of North Carolina Biography* (Chapel Hill: University of North Carolina Press, 1991), vol. 4, L–O, entry by John Macfie, 131.
2. Millie-Christine tombstone in the Welches Creek Community Cemetery in North Carolina.
3. Minnie McIver Brown, "Does Death Come On as a Peaceful Dream? Carolina Prodigy Is Remarkable Witness," Raleigh, N.C., *News and Observer*, Sunday, November 29, 1925, 1.

SCOTT JOPLIN

1. Susan Curtis, *Dancing to a Black Man's Tune: A Life of Scott Joplin* (Columbia: University of Missouri Press, 1994), 36.
2. Barbara Carlisle Bigelow, ed., *Contemporary Black Biography*, Profiles from the International Black Community (Detroit: Gale Research, Inc., 1994), vol. 6; "Scott Joplin" entry by Isaac Rosen, from Peter Gammond, *Scott Joplin and the Ragtime Era*, 151.
3. Edward A. Belin, "A Biography of Scott Joplin," The Scott Joplin International Ragtime Foundation website. http://www.scotjoplin.org/bio.html.
4. Melvin Drimmer, "Joplin's Treemonisha in Atlanta," *Phylon, The Atlanta University Review of Race and Culture* 34, no. 2, 199.

W. C. HANDY

1. W. C. Handy, *The Father of the Blues: An Autobiography* (New York: Macmillan Co., 1941), 16.

2. Ibid., 8.
3. Ibid., 16.
4. Ibid., 7.
5. Ibid., 5.
6. Ibid., 60.
7. Dorothy Scarborough, *On the Trail of Negro Folksongs* (Cambridge, Mass.: Harvard University Press, 1925), 265.
8. W. C. Handy Music Festival Brochure.
9. "The Evening Sun Goes Down," *Ebony* (June 1958), vol. XIII, no. 8, 97.

Gertrude "Ma" Rainey (Pridgett)

1. Darlene Clark Hine, ed., *Black Women in America: An Historical Encyclopedia* (New York: Carlson Publishing, Inc., 1993), 958.
2. Stamp on Black History, Index Website: http://library.advanced.org/10320/Stamps.htm (click on "Ma Rainey" entry in the "Second Age of Jazz").
3. Rock and Roll Hall of Fame "Ma" Rainey website: http://www.rockhall.com/induct/rainma.htm
4. Ibid.

Eubie Blake and Noble Sissle

1. Rose, Al, and Eubie Blake, *Eubie Blake* (New York: Schirmer Books, 1979), 8.
2. Eileen Southern, *Readings in Black American Music* (New York: W.W. Norton & Co., 1971), 224.

Francis Hall Johnson

1. "Colgate Hears Famous Choir," Oneida (N.Y.) *Dispatch*, January 24, 1934; from the Francis Hall Johnson Biographical file; the University Archives and Records Center, University of Pennsylvania, Philadelphia.
2. Charles Hobson, "Hall Johnson: Preserver of Negro Spirituals," *Crisis* 73, no. 9 (November 1966): 483.
3. Verna Arvey, "Hall Johnson and His Choir," *Opportunity*, 19 reprint edition (May 1941): 151; the Francis Hall Johnson Biographical file; the University Archives and Records Center, University of Pennsylvania, Philadelphia.
4. Charles Hobson, 485.

Bessie Smith

1. Middleton Harris, *The Black Book* (New York: Random House, 1974), 41.
2. Chris Albertson, *The Encyclopedia of Southern Culture*, Charles Reagan Wilson and William Ferris, eds. (Chapel Hill: University of North Carolina Press, 1989), 1084.

Marian Anderson

1. Marian Anderson, *My Lord, What a Morning* (1956; reprint, Madison: University of Wisconsin Press, 1992), 8.
2. Kosti Vehanen, *Marian Anderson, A Portrait* (New York: Whittlesey House, McGraw-Hill Book Co., 1941), 10.
3. Anderson, *My Lord, What a Morning*, 24.

4. Ibid., 144.
5. Ibid., 189.

Paul Robeson

1. Carlyle Douglas, "Farewell to a Fighter," *Ebony* (April 1976), 34.
2. Ibid.
3. Alden Whitman, "Paul Robeson Dead at 77; Singer, Actor and Activist," *New York Times*, January 24, 1976, 125, no. 43, 099, 1; as cited in the *New York Times Obituaries Index, 1969–1978* (New York: The New York Times Company, 1980), 162.

Duke Ellington

1. Duke Ellington, *Music Is My Mistress* (1973; reprint, New York: Da Capo, 1988), 9.
2. Ibid., 20.
3. Smithsonian Institution's National Museum of American History, Archives Center, Duke Ellington Collection #301, p. 2; website: http://www.si.edu/nmah/archives/d530lb.html
4. James Haskins, *Black Music in America: A History Through Its People* (1987; reprint, New York: HarperTrophy Edition, 1993), 90.
5. Ellington, 447.

Thomas Andrew Dorsey

1. Michael W. Harris, *The Rise of Gospel Blues: The Music of Thomas Andrew Dorsey in the Urban Church* (New York: Oxford University Press, 1992), xvii.
2. Ibid., Mahalia Jackson, with Evan McLeod Wylie, *Movin' On Up* (New York: Hawthorn Books, 1966), 60.
3. Harris., 22.
4. Ibid.
5. Ibid., 36.
6. Ibid.
7. "King of the Gospel Writers," *Ebony* (November 1962), 122.
8. Gwendolin Sims Warren, *Ev'ry Time I Feel the Spirit: 101 Best-Loved Psalms, Gospel Hymns, and Spiritual Songs of the African American Church* (New York: Henry Holt and Co., 1997), 178.

Louis "Satchmo" Armstrong

1. Gary Giddins, *Satchmo* (1988; reprint, New York: Da Capo Press, 1998), 48.
2. Louis Armstrong, *Satchmo: My Life in New Orleans* (1954; reprint, New York: Da Capo Press, 1986), 28.
3. Ibid., 51.
4. Giddins, 165.

Mahalia Jackson

1. Jules Schwerin, *Got to Tell It: Mahalia Jackson, Queen of Gospel* (New York: Oxford University Press, 1992), 26.
2. Schwerin, 30.
3. Ibid.

4. Mahalia Jackson, with Evan McLeod Wylie, *Movin' On Up* (New York: Hawthorn Books, 1966), 129.
5. Ibid.
6. Ibid., 36.
7. Schwerin, 62.
8. Ibid., 132.
9. Jackson, 80.
10. Ibid., 29.
11. Bill Morrison, "Blessed Assurance: Caesar Shines," *News & Observer* (Raleigh, N.C.) March 2, 1976, 3G.
12. Ibid.

ELLA FITZGERALD

1. Carolyn Wyman, *Ella Fitzgerald, Jazz Singer Supreme* (New York: Franklin Watts, 1993), 50.
2. Hettie Jones, *Big Star Fallin' Mama: Five Women in Black Music* (New York: The Viking Press, 1974), 91.

B.B. KING

1. B. B. King, with David Ritz, *Blues All Around Me* (New York: Avon Books, 1996), 19.
2. Ibid., 44.

CHUCK BERRY

1. Chuck Berry, *Chuck Berry, the Autobiography* (New York: Harmony Books, Isalee Publishing, 1987), 4.
2. http://www.rockhall.com/induct/berrchuc.html

RAY CHARLES

1. Ray Charles and David Ritz, *Brother Ray: Ray Charles' Own Story* (New York: Dial, 1978), 17.
2. Ibid., 164.
3. Irwin Stambler, ed., *The Encyclopedia of Pop, Rock and Soul* (New York: St. Martin's Press, 1974), 111.

JAMES BROWN

1. Shirelle Phelps, ed., *Contemporary Black Biography* (Detroit: Gale Research, Inc., 1997), vol. 15, 33.
2. James Brown with Bruce Tucker, *James Brown, The Godfather of Soul* (New York: Macmillan Publishing Co., 1986), 5.
3. Ibid., 264.
4. Phelps, 37.

DOUG AND FRANKIE QUIMBY

1. Daniel Gewertz, "Black History Alive in Singers Act," Boston Herald, April 12, 1991, S22.
2. Bruce Morgan, "In Georgia: Through the Gospel Grapevine," *Time*, September 12, 1981 (no page number listed).
3. Interview with the author, November 11, 1998.

4. Interview with the author.
5. Interview with the author.
6. Interview with the author.

Aretha Franklin

1. James Haskins, *Black Music in America: A History Through Its People* (1987; reprint, New York: HarperTrophy Edition, 1993), 157.
2. Ibid.

Jessye Norman

1. Jim Garvey, "The Journey from Bethlehem: The Making of a Diva" *Augusta* magazine 25, no. 6 (December 1998/January 1999), 32.
2. Ibid.
3. Ibid.
4. Jessie Carney Smith, ed., *Notable Black American Women* (Detroit: Gale Research, 1992), in Robert W. Stephens entry, "Jessye Norman," 809.
5. John Gruen, "An American Soprano Adds the Met to Her Roster," *New York Times*, September 18, 1983, 24.

Michael Jackson

1. J. Randy Taraborrelli, *Michael Jackson: The Magic and the Madness* (Secaucus, N.J.: Birch Lane Press, Carol Publishing Co., 1991), 7.
2. Ibid., 12.
3. Ibid., 17.

Queen Latifah

1. Queen Latifah, with Karen Hunter, *Ladies First: Revelations of a Strong Woman* (New York: William Morrow, 1999), 17.
2. Ibid., 55.
3. "Queen Latifah," cover story, *Jet* 95, no. 8 (January 25, 1999), 63.

BIBLIOGRAPHY

BOOKS

Adams, Russell L. *Great Negroes, Past and Present.* 1964. Reprint, Chicago: Afro-Am Publishing Co., 3rd ed., 1984.

Anderson, Marian. *My Lord, What a Morning: An Autobiography.* 1956. Reprint, Madison: University of Wisconsin Press, 1992.

Armstrong, Louis. *Satchmo: My Life in New Orleans.* 1954. Reprint, New York: Da Capo Press, 1986.

Berry, Chuck. *Chuck Berry:The Autobiography.* New York: Harmony Books, Isalee Publishing, 1987.

Charles, Ray, and David Ritz. *Brother Ray: Ray Charles' Own Story.* New York: Dial, 1978.

Colin, Sid. *Ella: The Life and Times of Ella Fitzgerald.* London: Elm Tree Books, 1987.

Curtis, Susan. *Dancing to a Black Man's Tune: A Life of Scott Joplin.* Columbia: University of Missouri Press, 1994.

Ellington, Duke. *Music Is My Mistress.* 1973. Reprint, New York: Da Capo Press, 1988.

Fernett, Gene. *Swing Out: Great Negro Dance Bands.* 1970. Reprint, New York: Da Capo Press, 1993.

Garland, Phyl. *The Sound of Soul.* Chicago: Henry Regnery Company, 1969.

Giddins, Gary. *Satchmo.* 1988. Reprint, New York: Da Capo Press, 1998.

Gourse, Leslie. *Aretha Franklin: Lady Soul.* New York: Franklin Watts, 1995.

Hamilton, Virginia. *Paul Robeson: The Life and Times of a Free Black Man.* New York: Harper and Row, 1974

Handy, W. C. *Father of the Blues: An Autobiography.* New York: Macmillan, 1941.

Hare, Maud Cuney. *Negro Musicians and Their Music.* Washington, D.C.: Associated Publishers, 1936.

Harris, Michael W. *The Rise of Gospel Blues: The Music of Thomas Andrew Dorsey in the Urban Church.* New York: Oxford University Press, 1992.

Harris, Middleton. *The Black Book.* New York: Random House, 1974.

Harris, Sheldon. *Blues Who's Who: A Biographical Dictionary of Blues Singers.* 1979. Reprint, New Rochelle, N.Y.: Da Capo Press; 1993.

Haskins, James. *Black Music in America: A History Through Its People.* 1987. Reprint, New York: HarperTrophy, 1993.

Haskins, James, and Kathleen Benson. *Scott Joplin.* Garden City, N.Y.: Doubleday, 1978.

Hayes, Roland. *My Songs: Afroamerican Religious Folk Songs.* Arranged and Interpreted. Boston: Little, Brown, 1948.

Heilbut, Anthony. *The Gospel Sound: Good News and Bad Times.* 1975. Reprint, New York: Limelight Edition, 1992.

Helander, Brock. *The Rock Who's Who.* New York: Schirmer Books, 1996.

Hine, Darlene Clark, ed. *Black Women in America: An Historical Encyclopedia.* Brooklyn, N.Y.: Carlson Publishing, 1993.

Jablonski, Edward. *The Encyclopedia of American Music.* Garden City, N.Y.: Doubleday, 1981.

Jackson, Mahalia, with Evan McLeod Wylie. *Movin' on Up.* New York: Hawthorn Books, 1966.

Jones, LeRoi. *Blues People: Negro Music in White America.* New York: William Morrow, 1963.

King, B. B., with David Ritz. *Blues All Around Me.* New York: Avon Books, 1996.

Kliment, Bud. *Ella Fitzgerald: First Lady of American Song.* Los Angeles: Melrose Square Publishing, 1989.

Latifah, Queen, with Karen Hunter. *Ladies First: Revelations of a Strong Woman.* New York: William Morrow, 1999.
Locke, Alain. *The Negro and His Music.* New York: Arno Press and the New York Times, 1969.
Mooney, Louise, ed. *Newsmakers.* Detroit: Gale Research, 1994.
Moore, Carman. *Somebody's Angel Child: The Story of Bessie Smith.* New York: Dell, Laurel Leaf edition, 1975.
Morgan, Tom, and William Barlow. *From Cakewalks to Concert Halls: An Illustrated History of African American Popular Music from 1895 to 1930.* Washington, D.C.: Elliott and Clark Publishing, 1992.
Nicholson, Stuart. *Ella Fitzgerald: A Biography of the First Lady of Jazz.* 1993. Reprint, New York: Da Capo Press, 1995.
Nolen, Rose M. *Sedalia's Ragtime Man.* Sedalia, Mo.: RoseMark Communications Publication, n.d.
Phelps, Shirelle, ed. *Contemporary Black Biography,* vol. 16. Detroit: Gale Research, 1998.
Rose, Al, and Eubie Blake. *Eubie Blake.* New York: Schirmer Books, a division of Macmillan, 1979.
Scarborough, Dorothy. *On the Trail of Negro Folksongs.* Cambridge: Harvard University Press, 1925.
Schwerin, Jules. *Got to Tell It: Mahalia Jackson, Queen of Gospel.* New York: Oxford University Press, 1992.
Sims, Janet L. *Marian Anderson: An Annotated Bibliography and Discography.* Westport, Conn.: Greenwood Press, 1981.
Smith, Eric. *Blacks in Opera: An Encyclopedia of People and Companies, 1873–1993.* Jefferson, N.C.: McFarland and Co., 1995.
Smith, Jessie Carney, ed. *Notable Black American Women.* Detroit: Gale Research, Inc., 1992.
Smythe, Mabel M., ed. *The Black American Reference Book.* Englewood Cliffs, N.J.: Prentice-Hall, 1976.
Southern, Eileen. *Biographical Dictionary of African American and African Musicians.* Westport, Conn.: Greenwood Press, 1982.
———. *Readings in Black American Music.* New York: W. W. Norton, 1971.
Stambler, Irwin, ed. *The Encyclopedia of Pop, Rock and Soul.* New York: St. Martin's Press. 1974.
Thompson, Oscar, ed. *The International Encyclopedia of Music and Musicians.* New York: Dodd, Mead, 1975.
Turner, Tina, with Kurt Loder. *I, Tina.* New York: Avon Books, 1987.
Vehanen, Kosti. *Marian Anderson: A Portrait.* New York: McGraw-Hill, 1941.
Warren, Gwendolin Sims. *Ev'ry Time I Feel the Spirit.* New York: Henry Holt and Company, 1997.
White, Charles, Richard Wayne Penniman, and Robert A. Blackwell. *The Life and Times of Little Richard, the Quasar of Rock.* New York: Harmony Books, 1984.
Wilson, Charles Reagan, and William Ferris, eds. *Encyclopedia of Southern Culture.* Chapel Hill: University of North Carolina Press. 1989.
Wyman, Carolyn. *Ella Fitzgerald, Jazz Singer Supreme.* New York: Franklin Watts, 1993.

Reference Works

Bigelow, Barbara Carlisle, ed. *Contemporary Black Biography: Profiles from the International Black Community.* vol. 2. Detroit: Gale Research, Inc., 1992.
———. Vol. 6.
———. Vol. 7.

Bonvente, Peter, ed. *Life: Forty Years of Rock and Roll.* New York: Time, Inc. vol. 15, no. 13, December 1, 1992.

Mabunda, L. Mpho, ed. *Contemporary Black Biography.* vol. 8. Detroit: Gale Research, Inc., 1995.

Magazine Articles

Bailey, Peter. "A Love Song to Eubie." *Ebony* 28, no. 9 (July 1973), 94.

Chambers, Lori. "Paul Robeson." *Rutgers* 78, no. 1 (Spring 1998).

Collins, Louise Mooney, and Frank Castronova, eds. *Newsmakers, 1996 Edition.* Detroit: Gale Research, 1997.

Daniel, David. "Norman Conquest." *Vogue* (March 1993), 428–430.

Douglas, Carlyle. "Paul Robeson: Farewell to a Fighter." *Ebony* (April 1976), 34.

Drimmer, Melvin. "Joplin's *Treemonisha* in Atlanta." *Phylon, the Atlanta University Review of Race and Culture* 34, no. 2, 199.

Ewey, Melissa. "Lauryn Hill: Hip-Hop's Hottest Star." *Ebony* 54, no. 7 (May 1999), 62.

Garvey, Jim. "The Journey from Bethlehem: The Making of a Diva." *Augusta* 25, no. 6 (December 1998/January 1999), 32.

Jenkins, Speight. "Jessye Norman's Conquests: From Lieder to 'Liebestod.' " *Ovation* (July 1981), p. 11.

"Lady from Philadelphia." *Ebony* 13 (March 1958), 32.

"Lauryn Hill Speaks Out on How Motherhood Made Her Sexy and Why She's Not a Diva." *Jet* 95, no. 10 (February 8, 1999).

"Perennial Diva." *New Yorker* (August 21, 1995), 58.

"Queen Latifah." Cover story. *Jet* 95, no. 8 (January 25, 1999).

"Roland Hayes: A Lifetime on the Concert Stage." *Ebony* 17, no. 11 (September 1962), 42–46.

"Standing His Ground." *Time* 26, no. 3. (April 1998), 39.

"The Swinging Aretha." *Ebony* 19, no. 5 (March 1964).

Newspaper Articles

Associated Press. " 'Satchmo' Called Hero for Integration Blast." *Grand Forks Herald* (North Dakota), September 21, 1957, 1.

Dornik, Verena. "Black Male Singers Are the 'Invisible Men' of Opera." *News & Observer* (Raleigh, N.C.), January 31, 1997, 5D.

Gruen, John. "An American Soprano Adds the Met to Her Roster." *New York Times,* September 18, 1983, 24.

Hasse, John Edward. "Bringing Out the Best in Ellington." Special to the *Washington Post,* April 11, 1999. Washington Post website: http://www.washingtonpost.com/

Henahan, Donal. "Jessye Norman—People Look at Me and Say 'Aïda.'" *New York Times,* January 21, 1973.

Holden, Stephen. "Ella Fitzgerald, the Voice of Jazz, Dies at 70." *New York Times,* June 16, 1996, 1.

Kozinn, Allan. "Contralto Marian Anderson Overcame Cruel Obstacles." *Oregonian* (Portland, Ore.), April 9, 1993, A14.

———. "Marian Anderson Is Dead at 96; Singer Shattered Racial Barriers." *New York Times,* April 9, 1993, 1.

Krebs, Albin. "Louis Armstrong, Jazz Trumpeter and Singer, Dies in His Home at 71." *New York Times,* July 7, 1971, 1.

New York Times Obituaries Index, 1969–1978. New York: The New York Times Company, 1980.

Offenburger, Chuck. "Simon Estes' Big Commitment." *Des Moines Sunday Register,* February 23, 1997, 1B.
Stabler, David. "Contralto Marian Anderson Dies at 96." *Oregonian* (Portland, Ore.), April 9, 1993, 1.
Wiley, Debora. "Simon Estes: No Bitterness Toward Iowa." *Des Moines Register,* May 26, 1991, 1.
Wilson, John S. "Armstrong Was Root Source of Jazz." *New York Times,* July 7, 1971, 41.
———. "Duke Ellington, a Master of Music, Dies at 75." *New York Times Obituaries Index,* 1969–1978. New York: The New York Times Company, 1980.

Other Sources

Willis, Allee. "In the Beginning: The World of Aretha Franklin, 1960–1961." New York: CBS, Inc., 1972. Album liner notes.

Internet Sites

http://cgi.pathfinder.com/time/magazine/1998/dom/980302/the_arts.music.soul_sist11.html
http://webhome.globalserve.net/ebutler website: "Neat Facts on Aretha"
http://imusic.com/showcase/urban/arethafranklin.html
http://www.rockhall.com/induct/franaret.html

PICTURE CREDITS

Page 8: courtesy of Photographs and Prints Division, Schomburg Center for Research in Black Culture, the New York Public Library/Astor, Lenox and Tilden Foundations; page 13: courtesy of the Amistad Research Center, Tulane University, New Orleans; page 18: courtesy of Photographs and Print Division, Schomburg Center for Research in Black Culture, the New York Public Library/Astor, Lenox and Tilden Foundations; page 22: courtesy of the Regional Museum of Spartanburg County, Spartanburg, S.C.; page 28: courtesy of Jim Haskins's collection; page 30: courtesy of the Kansas City Museum, Kansas City, Mo.; page 33: courtesy of Library of Congress, Washington, D.C.; page 40: courtesy of Photographs and Print Division, Schomburg Center for Research in Black Culture, the New York Public Library/Astor, Lenox and Tilden Foundations; page 44: courtesy of Archive Photos; page 47: courtesy of Photographs and Print Division, Schomburg Center for Research in Black Culture, the New York Public Library/Astor, Lenox and Tilden Foundations; page 50: courtesy of Collections of the Archives and Records Center, University of Pennsylvania, Philadelphia; page 51: courtesy of Carole Hall; page 53: courtesy of Photographs and Print Division, Schomburg Center for Research in Black Culture, the New York Public Library/Astor, Lenox and Tilden Foundations; pages 56 and 61: courtesy of Library of Congress, Washington, D.C.; page 65: courtesy of Photographs and Print Division, Schomburg Center for Research in Black Culture, the New York Public Library/Astor, Lenox and Tilden Foundations; page 68: courtesy of National Archives Washington, D.C.; pages 71 and 74: courtesy of William Gottlieb, the Library of Congress Collection, Washington, D.C.; page 77: courtesy of Reuters/Archive Photos; page 81: courtesy of Fisk University Library Special Collections, Nashville; page 88: courtesy of William Gottlieb, the Library of Congress Collection, Washington, D.C.; page 92: courtesy of Library of Congress, Washington, D.C.; pages 99 and 102; courtesy of William Gottlieb, the Library of Congress Collection, Washington, D.C.; page 104: courtesy of Panopticon Gallery, Boston; pages 109 and 114: courtesy of Archive Photos; page 116: courtesy of Zack E. Hamlett III; page 119: courtesy of Frank Driggs Collection/Archive Photos; page 124; courtesy of Georgia Sea Island Singers, Atlanta; page 128: courtesy of Arista Records; pages 133 and 136: courtesy of AP/Wide World Photos; page 139: courtesy of Archive Photos; page 143: courtesy of Epic Records, A Division of Sony Music; page 149: courtesy of AP/Wide World Photos.

INDEX